Charles H. Goren's

CONTRACT BRIDGE
for
BEGINNERS

A Simple Concise Guide for the Novice

(Including Point Count Bidding)

A Fireside Book
Published by
SIMON AND SCHUSTER

ISBN 0-671-21052-1
MANUFACTURED IN THE UNITED STATES OF AMERICA

42   43   44   45   46   47   48   49   50

To that fine, hard-working group—
THE BRIDGE TEACHERS—
who have done so much
to spread the pleasures of the game

TABLE OF CONTENTS

FOREWORD

IF YOU *have never played bridge before, I can promise that there is an exciting adventure in store for you.*

Bridge today enjoys an exalted position, though it was not always so. The attitude toward card games has varied considerably through the ages. Originally they were identified with games of chance, and as such were looked upon by large sections of humanity as instruments of the devil. It took generations to break down the resistance, and today Contract Bridge, the illustrious offspring of Whist, is characterized by men of letters, among them Somerset Maugham, as "the most entertaining game that the art of man has ever devised."

An intellectual pastime requiring no stake, and one which has been reduced largely to a contest of matching wits, Contract Bridge enjoys a prodigious following. It is now the game of the masses as well as those of higher estate. It is the game which provided an escape from the grim realities to those in command of our armed forces during the tense hours immediately preceding the Normandy invasion. It is the game which many schools are including in their curricula as a course in logic.

Naturally, in a work of this type I have made no pretense at completeness. I have stressed fundamentals and avoided exceptions in an effort to effect a smooth introduction to the game. At moments the elementary treatment may be tedious, but I hope it will hurt for only a moment. I am convinced that the more you learn about the game the better you'll like it, and I shall be very pleased if this little contribution will help you get off to a good start. After that, I hope we'll meet in one of the more advanced books.

CHARLES H. GOREN

CONTRACT BRIDGE
for
BEGINNERS

PRELIMINARIES

FOR THE purpose of this chapter I am proceeding upon the assumption that the reader is totally unfamiliar with the deck of playing cards. If in your case I have made an incorrect assumption, please do not, out of a sense of courtesy, linger over these pages. Simply skip this chapter on Preliminaries.

The Deck

Before embarking on the study of Contract Bridge one must acquaint oneself thoroughly with the values of the cards which make up the deck. The game can be played with only one deck of cards, but it is more convenient to use two separate packs. Only one pack is in use at a time, and while one is in use the other is being shuffled or mixed to be ready for the next deal. In order to avoid confusion it is better to employ decks with different colored backs.

The standard pack contains 52 cards. It is true that as you take them from the container you will find 54 cards; but two of them are Jokers, which are used in some games, but not in Bridge. So for the immediate future I suggest that you put them out to pasture.

The Four Suits

The deck is divided into four SUITS: Spades (♠), Hearts (♡), Diamonds (◇), Clubs (♣). Each suit contains 13 cards: Ace,

King, Queen, Jack, 10, 9, 8, 7, 6, 5, 4, 3, 2. In designating a card you specify first the number and then the suit.

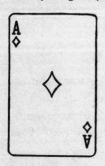

Ace of Diamonds   **King of Hearts**   **Four of Clubs**

There are some cards which are more frequently referred to by their nicknames. The three is usually called the TREY, and the two is almost universally designated as the DEUCE.

Rank of the Cards

Each card has its rank. The rank represents the ability to capture other cards of the same suit. The highest-ranking card is the Ace, which can capture any of the other twelve cards in that suit. The King, while it is outranked by the Ace and may be captured by it, has the ability to capture eleven other cards in that suit, from the Queen on down to the Deuce. Next to the Queen comes the Jack, and after that the numbers in descending order from the 10 down through the Deuce. The five highest-ranking cards (Ace, King, Queen, Jack, 10) are called HONOR CARDS. Their significance will become more apparent to you as we progress.

Assuming that you and your opponents are all playing cards of the same suit, any card which is higher in rank will capture any other card which is lower in rank. But as I indicated a moment ago, the question of rank does not come up unless you are playing cards of the same suit. Your Ace of Diamonds will capture someone else's King of Diamonds because it is higher in rank, but that same Ace of Diamonds will not capture someone else's Deuce of Clubs. To capture a Club you would need a higher-ranking Club.

In the preceding paragraphs we have been discussing the rank (capturing power) of cards where all players have played cards of the same suit. Now we come to a more complicated situation where all players are not able to play cards of the same suit. During the bidding period, which we shall take up in a subsequent chapter, one of the suits may be named by the highest bidder to be the TRUMP SUIT. When this is done, that suit becomes invested with certain trick-taking powers which the other suits do not possess. It becomes in a sense the privileged class. The special privilege of this suit is as follows: a player holding a trump card may use it to RUFF or TRUMP any card of some other suit. That means that if that player plays a card of the trump suit, he will capture the played cards of the other suits, even though they are of higher rank. The trump suit in effect has a veto power. It can veto a higher rank of some other suit. A trump card, however low in rank, will capture the highest-ranking card of any other suit. If Clubs are trump, the Deuce of Clubs will prevail over the Ace of Spades. The only cards which can beat the Deuce of Clubs (trumps) are the Clubs (trumps) of higher rank.

However, it may be pointed out at this time that players are at all times required to follow suit if they can. That is to say, if the first player plays a Spade, everyone else must play a Spade, if able to, and may not use a trump unless he has no Spades. If any player has no Spades he may trump, if he chooses, or he may throw a card of some other suit, in which case the four cards played are taken in by the one who played the highest card of the suit which was led. (These four cards constitute what is known as a TRICK.)

The suits also have ranks. Their rank is:

Spades ♠
Hearts ♡
Diamonds ◊
Clubs ♣

The Game

Contract Bridge is divided into two major parts: (1) the bidding; (2) the play. I shall temporarily refrain from discussing the bidding until I have given you some idea of the play, which in turn will simplify the problem of bidding. The bidding takes place at the beginning, but for the reasons outlined above we shall start with the mechanics of the play of the cards.

During the bidding there is an auction to determine the right to name the final trump. The rank of the suits has an important bearing on this bidding, and we shall discuss this presently.

The active participants at the Bridge table are always four players, but they do not play individually, for two of them are pitted against the two players sitting in the opposite direction, each partner facing the other partner. The partners share in the responsibility for anything done by either member of the partnership. All gains are credited to both members of the partnership, and all losses are charged in the same manner.

Partnerships are chosen by drawing cards. A deck of cards is spread face down on the table and each player draws one card. The two players drawing the high cards become partners. They sit facing each other and play against the other two. If two cards of the same denomination are drawn, the higher is determined by the rank of the suits and for this purpose the suits rank: Spades, Hearts, Diamonds and Clubs.

The player who cuts the highest card becomes the dealer and has the choice of seats and cards. Remember, Contract Bridge should be played with two decks with different backs, and while one partner deals, his partner should shuffle the other deck for the next dealer and place the deck to his own right so that it will be readily available for the next dealer.

The dealer presents the cards to his right-hand opponent for the CUT. The cut is merely the process of lifting off a portion of the deck and placing it on the table toward the dealer, just beside the bottom portion. However, each portion must contain at least four cards. That is to say, the player making the cut must remove at least four cards or at most forty-eight. The dealer then completes the cut by placing the bottom portion on top of the portion which the cutter has removed. The dealer then deals thirteen cards to each player, one at a time in a clockwise direction, that is, to his left. Each player then picks up his thirteen cards. This distribution of the cards is known as the DEAL.

After the cards have been dealt, there is a period during which the BIDDING takes place. This bidding is known as the AUCTION. When a player makes a bid, he offers to win a certain number of tricks.

When a player makes the highest bid, he and his partner win the contract, and we may for purposes of identification refer to them as the CONTRACTING SIDE. They have just contracted to win the number of tricks specified in their final bid.

Then comes the play period. One of the contracting players is called the DECLARER. He might be considered the active partner. The other member is called the DUMMY. The declarer is always that member of the partnership who first mentioned the trump suit in which the hand is to be played (not necessarily the last bidder).

When the bidding ends, the player to the left of the declarer places one of his thirteen cards face up on the table. This is known as the OPENING LEAD, which inaugurates the play of the hand. The opening leader is not restricted in his choice. He may choose any one of his thirteen cards. And it will do no harm to repeat that all players must follow suit if they can. If these players hold more than one card in the suit led, they may choose to play on any particular trick any one of the cards held. They need not beat any card played to the trick, unless they choose to do so. If a player cannot follow suit, he may play any card in his hand without restriction. He need not trump, but he may if he so desires.

After the opening lead, the partner of the declarer spreads his thirteen cards upon the table, and this hand becomes the dummy. The declarer chooses each and every card that is to be played from dummy. He plays both his hand and the dummy hand, but the defending players play their own hands. The cards are played to each trick in the player's proper turn. No card may be played out of turn. When each player has played, there will be four cards on the table, and these are called a TRICK. Of the four cards played to the trick, one card will have winning rank and will capture that trick. The player whose card has captured the trick has the right to lead to the next trick; and the same process is continued until all thirteen cards have been played.

Let us observe the mechanics of trick-taking with a few illustrations.

We shall assume that the bidding has been completed and play is about to begin. For purposes of identification, we shall refer to the players by directions, as though we were looking down upon the table as we would upon a map. North is the upper part of the diagram; East is to the right; South at the lower part of the picture; and West to the left. This map is as natural to a Bridge player as a beard is to Uncle Sam. For the purpose of our discussion, South will be declarer and naturally, therefore, North will be the dummy.

The first play, known as the opening lead, has been made by the player to declarer's left—that is, West.

NORTH (Dummy)

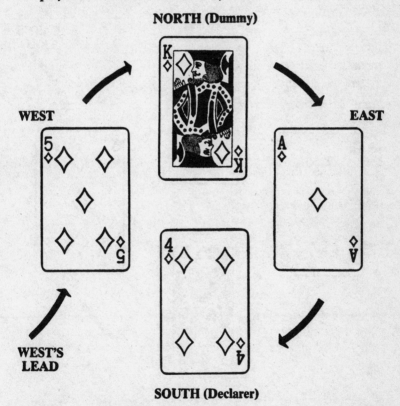

WEST

EAST

WEST'S LEAD

SOUTH (Declarer)

North and South are the contractors and are partners against East and West. Note that a card has been played by each of the

four players, who have played in rotation (clockwise), starting
with West. The four cards are at the moment face up on the table
and are about to be picked up by East on behalf of his partnership.* These four cards (a trick) belong to East and West. In
other words, they have won the first trick because East played
the highest card of the trick and therefore captured the others.

Play then proceeds to trick number two. Inasmuch as East won

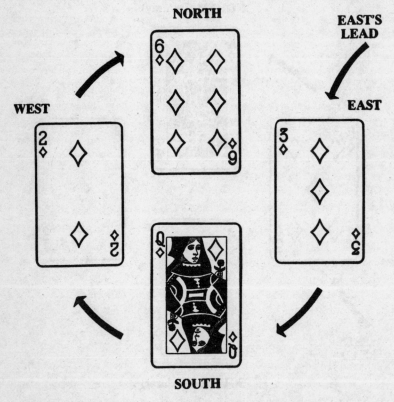

* For the sake of convenience, one member keeps all the tricks taken in by
his partner and himself.

the first trick (though it goes to the partnership credit), he plays first (that is, he leads) to the next trick.

Observe that East led the 3 of Diamonds to trick two. The other three hands played in rotation in a clockwise direction. South played the Queen of Diamonds, West the Deuce of Diamonds, and North the 6 of Diamonds. The Queen of Diamonds was the highest card played to this trick and therefore captured the other three cards. The trick is therefore won by the player who played this high card, namely South. He gathers up the four cards and places the trick face down in front of him. Now at the end of the second trick each side has won a trick, and play proceeds in this manner until all the cards have been played. Consequently, there will always be exactly thirteen tricks in each hand.

It has been pointed out that the winner of each trick must lead to the next trick and that play always proceeds in a clockwise direction. A player may not put down his card until it is his turn to play. If West is the leader, East may not play until after North has played, and South must wait for East to play before he puts down his card.

It might be profitable to repeat at this time the FOLLOW-SUIT RULE, which provides as follows: Whereas the leader to each trick has his own complete choice as to which card to play, the other three players are restricted in their choice. They must follow suit if possible—that is to say, they must play cards of the same suit as the card which the leader played. They may play high cards or low cards at their own discretion, but they must follow suit if able to do so. However, if a player has no cards of that suit, he is at liberty to play any card he chooses.

We have previously made a brief reference to the dummy (declarer's partner). After the opening lead dummy spreads his hand (13 cards), arranged in suits, face up on the board before him. Thereafter he remains silent—dumb. Declarer indicates what card he is to play whenever it becomes dummy's turn to play. However, declarer must observe all the rules in regard to dummy's hand, just as he does with his own. The dummy must play in proper turn (though the cards are actually selected by declarer); the dummy must follow suit, if possible; and, when a trick is won in dummy, the lead to the next trick must come from dummy's hand.

Tricks can be won not only with high cards (though most tricks are won that way) but also with low cards. In the illustrations we have examined thus far all players followed suit, and the trick went to that player who played the highest card. A 7 might win a trick if all other players put down smaller cards, but it would take the Ace to win a trick if one of the other players put down a King.

Winning Tricks by Using Trumps (Ruffing)

We have not yet come to the subject of the selection of a trump suit, but it has been pointed out that one of the distinctive features of the game of Bridge is that in many hands a suit in due course becomes chosen as the trump suit and enjoys a certain superiority over the others. Every card of the trump suit is vested with a superior trick-taking power. It is known as the RUFFING power (or trumping power), which a player may exercise whenever he is unable to follow suit.

A player who has no cards of the suit which has been led may ruff, or trump, by playing any card of the trump suit. If he is the only one who has played a trump, he wins the trick regardless of the size of his trump. In other words, the Deuce of trumps will capture the Ace of some other suit, provided the player who produces the Deuce of trumps has no more of the suit which has been led.

NORTH

WEST   **EAST**

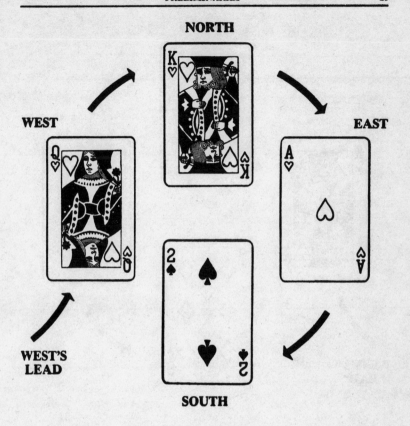

**WEST'S
LEAD**

SOUTH

Spades are trumps. West leads the Queen of Hearts; North attempts to capture with the King of Hearts; East beats this with the Ace of Hearts. But South, who has no Hearts, wins the trick with the Deuce of Spades, which is trump.

If more than one player uses a trump on any particular trick, the player who contributes the highest trump wins the trick. In other words, a trump can be captured by a higher-ranking trump. Observe the following illustration:

NORTH

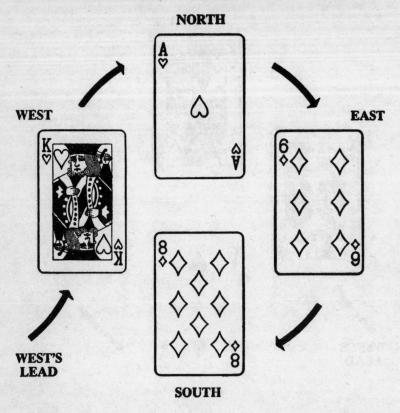

WEST

EAST

**WEST'S
LEAD**

SOUTH

Diamonds are trumps. West leads the King of Hearts; North follows suit with the Ace of Hearts; East, who has no Hearts, trumps (ruffs) with the 6 of Diamonds, which are trump. South also has no hearts, so he may play a trump if he chooses. He does choose to play the 8 of Diamonds, a higher trump, and therefore wins the trick. South is said to have won the trick by *over*-ruffing.

When a player is unable to follow suit, he may trump or he may play a card of some other suit. If he plays a trump, he is said to have ruffed. If he plays a card of some other suit, he is said to have made a DISCARD. The discard has no trick-taking power; therefore, the rank of the discard is immaterial. Any trick that does not contain a trump is won by the hand which plays the highest card of the suit led.

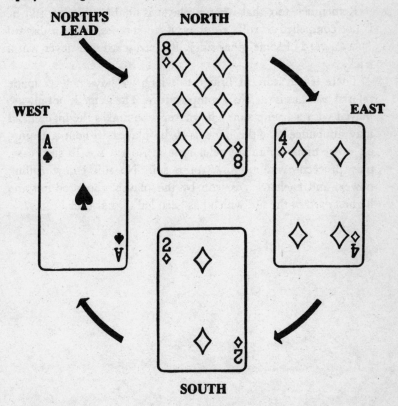

Hearts are trumps. North leads the 8 of Diamonds. East and South follow suit. West has no Diamonds and also has no trumps. He discards the Ace of Spades. North's 8 of Diamonds wins the trick. It is the highest card of the suit which was first led to that trick.

When a trump is led, the other three players must follow suit if they are able to. In other words, the follow-suit rule applies to trumps as well as to the other suits.

Remember that a player may not ruff if he is able to follow suit.

Remember, too, that when a player is unable to follow suit he is not compelled to ruff. He may, if he chooses, make a discard (play a card of some other suit). But a discard can never win a trick.

There is a feature of Bridge to which we have not yet made reference. That is the No Trump feature. The game is not always played with a trump suit. The player who makes the highest bid may announce that the hand is to be played without a trump, or, as we more commonly refer to it, at NO TRUMP. In such case, play proceeds without any trump suit. No suit enjoys ruffing power, and each trick is won by the player who produces the highest card of the suit which has been led to that trick.

CHAPTER II

THE MECHANICS OF BIDDING

LET US REVERT now to the time when the cards have just been dealt and each player has thirteen cards. We approach the time for bidding. This is known as the AUCTION. It is conducted in the manner of an auction. The highest bidder and his partner win the right to play the hand as contractors, and the highest bidder designates the trump suit (or No Trump).

The dealer is the first to speak during the auction. He may make a bid or he may pass. Whichever he does, it then becomes the turn of the player to his left and continues on around the table in clockwise rotation. The bidding ends when the highest bid has been made and is followed by three passes, which means that the remaining three players decline the opportunity to overbid the final bidder. The highest bid designates the contract at which the hand is to be played.

Since each player is dealt thirteen cards, there are thirteen tricks which can be won or lost. (Each of the four players in turn places a card upon the table; each of these groups of four cards is known as a "trick.") The lowest legal bid is to win one more trick than the other side wins, and out of thirteen the bare majority is seven. So that a contract to win seven tricks is the lowest legal bid. The highest possible contract is one which offers to win thirteen tricks.

For the sake of simplicity, the first six tricks which the bidder undertakes to win are not calculated in the bid, for only the tricks in excess of six constitute a majority. The first six tricks are referred to as BOOK. A bid of 3 Spades is a commitment to win nine tricks with Spades as trump. A bid of 7 Hearts is an offer to win all thirteen tricks with Hearts as trump. A player is never legally bound to bid. He may PASS whenever he chooses, and he may subsequently enter the auction, at his proper turn, if he sees fit to do so.

Let us examine an illustrative auction. Imagine the four players to be seated so that each player represents a direction on the map. South drew the highest card and became the dealer. He distributed the cards one at a time until each player had thirteen. Inasmuch as he was the dealer, he has the first chance to bid or pass. South carefully examined his cards and decided that he did not wish to make an offer to win seven tricks so he passed. The turn to bid then goes to West in a clockwise direction. West decided to bid 1 Heart. That is to say, he offered to win seven tricks with Hearts as trumps. Naturally, he does not expect to win all seven tricks in his own hand, but expects to get some help from his partner. West is now known as the OPENING BIDDER. The opening bidder is the one who makes the first bid of the auction. A pass is not regarded as a bid.

It is now North's turn to speak. If he wishes to bid, he must make some bid higher than which has just been made by West. West, you recall, just bid one Heart. North happens to have five Spades which are headed by the Ace and King, and a King in one of the other suits. He wishes to contest the bid of 1 Heart and may do so by bidding 1 Spade (an offer to win seven tricks with Spades as trumps). This is a higher bid than 1 Heart because Spades rank higher than Hearts in the bidding scale. Note that if North happened to have a Diamond suit instead of the Spade suit, he would be unable to bid 1 Diamond, for Hearts rank higher than Diamonds. If he wishes to enter the auction, he would have to bid 2 Diamonds. Two of any suit outbids one of any other suit.

Now it is East's turn. His partner, West, has bid 1 Heart. North, his opponent, has made a higher bid of 1 Spade. (This is known as an overcall.) East has very little of value in his hand, so he passes. It is now South's turn. Though he passed the first time, he is permitted to enter the auction now if he chooses. He has some help for partner with Spades as trump and decides to bid 2 Spades. This is called a RAISE, and it constitutes an offer to win eight tricks with Spades as trumps. West passes, North passes and East passes. This concludes the auction, and 2 Spades is the final bid. Whenever a bid is followed by three consecutive passes, the auction is over.

North and South, by making the final bid (2 Spades), gained the right to play as contractors. And the suit named in the final bid (Spades in this case) becomes trump. Though South made the final bid, nevertheless North is the declarer and plays the hand, because he is the member of the team who first named the suit (Spades).

A player is never legally bound to bid. He may pass whenever he chooses, and he may subsequently enter the auction if he sees fit to do so.

Doubles

When a side which has contracted to win a certain number of tricks fails to do so, there is a penalty. Suppose the bid was 4 Hearts. This was a contract to win ten tricks (four more than the book, which consists of the first six tricks), and after the play is over it develops that declarer succeeded in winning only nine tricks. He is known to have been SET one trick on his contract, or, as it is described more colloquially, he is "down one." If he had succeeded in winning only eight tricks, he would be down two.

The penalty for being set is a certain number of points which are awarded to the opposition. (See page 33 for scoring table.)

If, as an adversary of the bidder, you believe that he will be unable to make his bid, you may DOUBLE. This has the effect of increasing the amount of the penalty if the contract is set; but, on the other hand, if the contract is fulfilled against your expectation, the opponents' reward for making the hand will be correspondingly increased. (Again, see page 33 for scoring table.) The double may be made only when it is that player's turn to bid. In other words, a double is a BID.

If a player has been doubled, he may, if he chooses, REDOUBLE. (The redouble also must be made in turn.) This again doubles the amount of points involved. The right to redouble, when it is his turn to bid, is also vested in the partner of the player whose bid has been doubled.

CHAPTER III

HOW TO SCORE

AT THIS POINT, I prefer not to indulge in an exhaustive study of scoring. It is largely arbitrary and the reader will find the information in any scoring table which is readily available.

The object of the game of Bridge is to score more points than your opponents. You may score points as declarer (offensively) by fulfilling your contracts or bids, and you may score points (defensively) by preventing the opponents from fulfilling their contracts. Your opponents are penalized a certain number of points for every trick by which they are set.

In bidding offensively, the most important goal is the scoring of a GAME. Game in this sense is a technical term. You achieve a game when you have scored 100 or more points for fulfilling your own bids. These are sometimes called below-the-line points, because that is where they are recorded on the score pad. Only the points which you score by making your own contracts may be counted toward game. If you defeat an adverse contract by 100 points, that would not constitute a game. Such points are known as above-the-line points, for that is where they are recorded on the score pad.

Game may be scored either in one hand, or by the accumulation of the necessary points over several hands. If you have become declarer and have succeeded in fulfilling your contract, the tricks that you have bid for are scored as follows:

If Spades or Hearts are trump, you score 30 points for each trick taken in addition to your book (first six tricks). If Diamonds or Clubs are trump, you score 20 points for each trick over your book. If the contract is No Trump, you score 40 points for the first trick over your book and 30 points for each additional trick that you take.

When a side scores a game by making 100 such points, that game is over, and both opponents start again in an effort to make another game.

A game can be made in one hand if you bid and make 3 No Trump (40 + 30 + 30 = 100), 5 Clubs or Diamonds (5 × 20 = 100), 4 Hearts or Spades (4 × 30 = 120).* It can be made in two hands, as follows: On the first hand you bid and make 2 Spades, scoring 60 points below the line. On the next hand your opponents bid and make 2 No Trump. They have scored 70 points toward game (below the line). On the third hand you bid and make 3 Clubs, scoring 60 points. That gives you 120 trick points below the line, and you have a game. Now, both sides try for the next game. The 70 points scored by the opponents will not count toward the next game, though they will receive credit for those points when the final score is computed.

Extra Tricks

We have observed that the points scored below the line are those for tricks which have been BID FOR and made. Sometimes the declarer will win more tricks than he has contracted for. For example, he bids 2 Spades, a commitment to win eight tricks, and actually takes ten tricks. The ninth and tenth tricks are called OVERTRICKS. The points for these overtricks (60 points) are scored above the line, but do not count toward game. If you bid for 2 No Trump and make ten tricks, you have fulfilled your

---

* Note that it takes only ten tricks to make game in Spades or Hearts, which are known as the MAJOR SUITS, whereas it takes eleven tricks to make game in Clubs and Diamonds, which are known as the MINOR SUITS.

contract to win eight tricks and made two overtricks. You score these "bid" tricks (70 points) below the line, and the two over-tricks (60 points) above the line.

Bonuses

RUBBER BONUS

When a side scores two games, it is said to have won the RUBBER and receives a designated bonus. If your side wins both games, while the adversaries have not scored a game, your bonus is 700 points. If you win the rubber (two games), but the opponents have in the meantime won a game, your bonus is 500 points.

SLAM BONUS

When you bid for all the tricks and make them, you have scored a GRAND SLAM.

When you bid for all but one of the tricks, and are successful, you receive the bonus for a SMALL SLAM.

You must fulfill your contract in order to be eligible for the bonus. If you bid for a grand slam and make twelve tricks, you have not scored a small slam. You have been set one on your grand-slam contract.

THE BONUS FOR HONORS

This bonus is awarded for the mere possession of certain honors. An honor card is Ace, King, Queen, Jack, 10. Possession of any four honors *in the trump suit* carries with it a bonus of 100 points above the line, and possession of all five honors yields a bonus of 150 points. The honors must be held in one hand. If they are divided between the two hands, there is no bonus. Honors in a suit other than trump do not carry a bonus.

When the contract is No Trump, possession of all four aces in one hand carries a bonus of 150 points.

The honor bonus is awarded for mere possession. Therefore, it may accrue to either side, whether the honors are held by dummy or by either defender.

Vulnerability

As soon as you score a game, you become VULNERABLE. That means that losses incurred by you become increased, but some of the bonuses also become increased. If you succeed in making a small slam (a contract to win twelve tricks) when you are not vulnerable, you receive a bonus of 500 points. But if you bid and make a small slam when you are vulnerable, the bonus is 750. Similarly, a grand slam (a contract to win all thirteen tricks) not vulnerable yields 1000 points, but when vulnerable the yield is 1500. At the end of the rubber, a new rubber is started, and both sides are again not vulnerable.

The only bonuses available to defenders are for setting their opponents. When declarer fails in his contract, but is not doubled, he loses to the opponents 50 points per trick when not vulnerable and 100 points per trick when vulnerable. If the declarer is doubled, the penalties are higher. When not vulnerable, he pays 100 points for the first undertrick and 200 for each subsequent trick. When vulnerable, he pays 200 for the first trick and 300 for each subsequent trick. These points are scored above the line.

When declarer fulfills a doubled contract, the trick value of those tricks which he has bid for are doubled for purposes of scoring below the line.

Suppose, for example, the contract were 2 Spades. The most that declarer could score below the line is 60 points, no matter how many tricks he wins, so he cannot make game on this hand. But if an opponent doubles the bid, the value of Spade tricks increases from 30 to 60. A contract of 2 Spades doubled is, therefore, a bid to take 120 points worth of tricks. The result is scored below the line and therefore yields game. A contract of 2 Spades or 2 Hearts doubled is a game contract, but a contract of 2 Diamonds doubled would not produce game, for that would yield only 80 points (two times 40) below the line.

Doubling affects the value of overtricks. When declarer makes overtricks at a doubled contract, he receives 100 points per trick if not vulnerable, and 200 per trick if vulnerable, scored above the line. He also receives a bonus of 50 points not vulnerable and 50 points vulnerable, above the line, for making a doubled contract. Redoubling doubles these doubled values.

Scoring Table

Trick Score

Tricks bid for and made count toward game:

	Not Doubled	Doubled	Redoubled
Each trick over 6 (Book): Spades	30	60	120
Hearts	30	60	120
Diamonds	20	40	80
Clubs	20	40	80
No Trump—first trick over 6 (Book):	40	80	160
Each additional trick over 6 (Book):	30	60	120

These points are scored below the line.

Tricks over 6 made but not bid for do not count toward game:

	Not Vulnerable Trick Value	Vulnerable Trick Value
Undoubled, each		
Doubled, each	100	200
Redoubled, each	200	400

First side to score 100 points in trick-score wins game.

Having made game, a side is vulnerable.

First side to win two games wins the rubber.

For winning rubber, if opponents have no game	700
For winning rubber, if opponents have game	500
If rubber is unfinished, for winning game	300
If game is unfinished, for having a part-score	50

Premiums

	Not Vulnerable	Vulnerable
For bidding and making Small Slam (12 tricks)	500	750
For bidding and making Grand Slam (13 tricks)	1000	1500
For holding four trump honors in one hand	100	100
For holding five trump honors in one hand	150	150
For holding four Aces in one hand at No Trump	150	150
For making any doubled or redoubled contract	50	50

Penalties

If declarer fails to make his contract, opponents score:

	Not Vulnerable			Vulnerable		
	Not Doubled	Doubled	Redoubled	Not Doubled	Doubled	Redoubled
1 Down	50	100	200	100	200	400
2 Down	100	300	600	200	500	1000
3 Down	150	500	1000	300	800	1600
Add for each additional trick down	50	200	400	100	300	600

These points are scored above the line.

To aid in forming the habit of scoring properly, let us examine a sample scoring sheet:

WE	THEY	
	800	◄HAND (7)
HAND (8)► 500	60	◄HAND (6)
HAND (5)► 50	100	◄HAND (4)
HAND (1)► 60	30	◄HAND (2)
HAND (1)► 60	70	◄HAND (2)
HAND (3)► 40		
	120	◄HAND (6)
HAND (8)► 100		
810	1180	
	− 810	
	370	

THEY win by 370, though WE won rubber game.

Hand (1): WE bid 2 Spades and made 4. Scored below the line were 60 points toward game—only the tricks which were bid for (2 × 30 = 60). The overtricks were scored above the line.

Hand (2): THEY bid 2 No Trump, and though they made 3, did not score a game, for only 70 points' worth of tricks were bid for (40 for the first trick at No Trump, and 30 for the second). Therefore, only 70 points are scored below the line, and the other 30 above the line.

Hand (3): WE bid 1 No Trump and just fulfilled contract, yielding 40 points below the line. This, combined with the previously earned 60 points, yields 100 and gives WE the first game. A line is now drawn under the 40, and a new game is started. THEY no longer have the benefit of having 70 below the line for the next game, which starts from scratch; but, when the final score is computed, those 70 points will go to their credit. WE have now become vulnerable.

Hand (4): WE bid 4 Spades and succeeded in winning only nine tricks. WE were therefore set one trick. Since WE are vulnerable and not doubled, the penalty is 100 points, which is scored in favor of THEY above the line.

Hand (5): THEY bid 3 Clubs and were defeated by one trick. Since THEY are not vulnerable and were not doubled, the penalty is only 50 points, which is scored in favor of WE above the line.

Hand (6): THEY bid 4 Spades and made 6. Thus THEY score 120 below the line (4 x 30) and 60 (2 x 30), for the overtricks, above the line. This produces game, and a line is drawn below the 120. THEY have just become vulnerable, and both sides are in that condition.

Hand (7): WE bid 3 No Trump. THEY doubled, WE took only six tricks (our book). WE were therefore down three vulnerable. This gives THEY 800 points above the line.

Hand (8): WE bid 3 No Trump and this time made nine tricks. This gives WE 100 points below the line (40+30+30) and scores game. This is the second game of the rubber for one side, so the rubber is concluded, and a bonus of 500 points above the line is awarded to WE for winning the rubber. The points are now added up.

THEY have scored 1180, and WE have scored 810. THEY consequently win the rubber by 370 points. Notice that THEY are the winners, even though WE won the rubber game.

CHAPTER IV

WHAT SHALL I BID?

Valuation

BIDDING IS NOTHING more nor less than estimating how many tricks you will be able to win in the play. Such estimates cannot soundly be made without a knowledge of the value of high cards. For the purpose of evaluation, we assign certain numerical values to each of the face cards, and here is the table:

Ace	4 Points
King	3 Points
Queen	2 Points
Jack	1 Point
The entire pack contains 40 points	

If the high cards were equally distributed among the four players, each player would hold 10 points. That is to say, a holding of 10 points constitutes an average hand. If you wish to open the bidding, you should have better than an average hand, because you are undertaking to win more tricks than your adversaries. (A bid of 1 Club is a contract to win seven tricks, with Clubs as trump.)

It is to be observed that we can value our hand in two ways.

If we intend to play at No Trump, we count only our high cards. But if we intend to play with a suit as trump, we count our high cards as well as other factors, which we call DISTRIBU-TION—a phrase which will be interpreted for you at this point. At a suit contract we may win tricks with high cards, by trumping and also by building up little cards into winners late in the play.

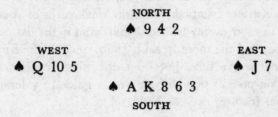

NORTH
♠ 9 4 2

WEST
♠ Q 10 5

EAST
♠ J 7

♠ A K 8 6 3
SOUTH

To illustrate let us examine this diagram. We are showing only part of the complete deal, that part which contains the Spade suit. In high cards alone South has 7 points and can win two quick tricks with the Ace and King. You will observe, however, that South will eventually win four tricks with his Spades. Let us examine the mechanics by which he does so.

Trick 1. South plays the Ace, West the 5, North the 2, and East the 7. South wins the trick.

Trick 2. South plays the King, West the 10, North the 4, and East the Jack. South wins the trick.

Trick 3. South plays the 3, West the Queen, North the 9, and East, who has no more Spades, plays a card of some other suit.
West wins the trick.

Trick 4. West leads a card of some other suit which South is able to win.

South now plays the 8 and 6 of Spades, and since no one else has any Spades, and we are presuming that trumps have been drawn (or that we are playing at No Trump) the 8 and 6 of Spades are commanding cards and win two tricks.

If your thirteen cards are distributed 4-3-3-3, there are no little cards to build into tricks; but if your hand contains a six-card suit, let us say your hand is distributed 6-3-3-1, you may expect to win tricks eventually with the small cards of your six-card suit. The more evenly balanced your hand is, the less powerful will it be; and the more freakish (unbalanced), the stronger you will find it. We have just been discussing distribution. It is now my purpose to provide you with a guide to valuing the distributional features of your hand.

When you have no cards of a particular suit, we call it a VOID. When you have only one card of a suit, we call it a SINGLETON. When you have only two cards of a suit, we refer to it as a DOUBLETON.

When you value your hand for the purpose of opening the bidding in a suit, you count first your high cards, then add 1 point for each doubleton, 2 points for each singleton, and 3 points if your hand contains a void.

Examples:

♠ A Q x x x	(6)	♠ A Q x x x	(6)
♡ A 10 x x x	(4)	♡ A 10 x x x	(4)
◇ x x	(1)	◇ x x x	
♣ x	(2)	♣ none	(3)

This hand has a value of
13 points.

This hand has a value of
13 points.

♠ A x x x   (4)
♡ K x   (4)
(3 for King; 1 for doubleton)
◇ A K J x x   (8)
♣ x x   (1)

This hand has a value of
17 points.

Opening the Bidding

If you wish to open the bidding with one of a suit, your hand must be above average in strength. We have recently observed that an average hand is worth 10 points. How much more than an average hand must you have before you may risk bidding one in a suit? The answer is a King above average, which amounts to 13 points. If you have this much, you *may* open the bidding. Sometimes with 13 points you may not feel like opening the bidding, but if you have 14 points or more, you should consider it your duty to bid one of some suit.*

Which suit should you bid? The suit which you select must be what we call a BIDDABLE SUIT. The first requirement is that it must contain at least four cards. Suits of three-card length must not be bid. Remember that when you have thirteen cards you are bound to have one suit which contains at least four cards. But any four cards do not constitute a biddable suit. The suit must be headed by some high cards. If you have 10-7-6-4, that is not a biddable suit. The weakest four-card suit which opener is permitted to bid is one headed by at least the Queen and Jack. In other words, *your four-card trump suit must contain at least 3*

---

* This may be an appropriate time to point out that when you open with one of a suit and your partner bids some new suit in response, his bid is forcing upon you for one round; that is to say, you must bid at least once more.

high-card points in the suit itself. The following four-card suits
are biddable:

Q J x x   K x x x.   A x x x   K J x x

A five-card suit is biddable even though it contains less high-
card strength in the suit. Any five-card suit is biddable if it contains a "face card" (Ace, King, Queen, or Jack), so that these
suits are biddable:

J x x x x   Q x x x x   K x x x x

Any six-card suit is biddable, even if it contains no high card.
8-6-5-4-3-2 is a biddable suit provided, of course, the hand itself
contains enough points to justify an opening bid.

It is important to determine how many points it will take in
the combined hands (your hand and your partner's) to produce
game. Experience has shown that it takes the equivalent of two
opening bids to produce game, and an opening bid is considered
basically to be about 13 points. So, if the partnership possesses
26 points, however divided between the partners, there should be
game in the hand. Another way I have chosen to state this principle is: *An opening bid facing an opening bid will usually produce game.*

Which Suit to Bid First

When you have more than one biddable suit, it is important
to make the proper choice for the opening bid. The most important consideration is the length of the suits.

If the suits are of unequal length, bid the longer one first.

If you have two five-card suits, you should bid first the higher ranking. Recall that Spades rank higher than Hearts, Hearts are higher than Diamonds, and Diamonds are higher than Clubs.

If you have more than one four-card suit, employ the following principle: Look for the shortest suit in your hand (singleton or doubleton) and bid first that suit which ranks next below your singleton or doubleton. If the suit below is not biddable, bid the next suit below that. Where your singleton is Clubs, open with 1 Spade.

For example:

♠ x x ♡ A Q x x ◇ A K J x ♣ x x x

Bid 1 Heart, the suit below the doubleton. If partner bids 2 Clubs, your rebid is 2 Diamonds, permitting partner to return to 2 Hearts cheaply.

♠ x x ♡ x x x ◇ K Q J x ♣ A K J x

Bid 1 Diamond (not 1 Club). The doubleton is Spades. The suit below is Hearts; but since your Heart suit is not biddable, bid the next suit below that.

♠ A K x x ♡ x x ◇ A K x x ♣ J x x

Bid 1 Diamond, the suit below the doubleton.

♠ A K x x ♡ J x x ◇ A K x x ♣ x x

Bid 1 Spade. The doubleton is Clubs; the suit below Clubs for the purpose of this rule is Spades.

EXAMPLES OF OPENING BIDS

(A)	(B)	(C)
♠ A Q 10 x x	♠ A K Q 10	♠ A x x
♡ A x	♡ J 10 x x	♡ A Q J 9 x x
◇ x x x	◇ K x	◇ x x
♣ x x x	♣ Q 10 x	♣ x x

(D)	(E)	(F)
♠ A K J x	♠ A x	♠ x
♡ A 9 x	♡ 9 x x x x x	♡ A K 10 x
◇ x x x	◇ A 10 x	◇ A 9 x x
♣ x x x	♣ A x	♣ J x x x

(G)	(H)	(I)
♠ A Q J x	♠ J x x	♠ Q 10 x x x
♡ x x	♡ A K x x	♡ A K x x x
◇ A Q x x x	◇ x x	◇ K x
♣ x x	♣ A Q x x	♣ x

(A) Pass. This hand is worth only 11 points (10 in high cards and 1 for the doubleton).

(B) Bid 1 Spade. This hand is worth 16 points valued at a suit (15 in high cards and 1 for the doubleton Diamond).

(C) Bid 1 Heart. This hand is worth 13 points (11 in high cards, 1 for the doubleton Diamond, and 1 for the doubleton Club). 13-point hands should always be opened when they contain a good five- or six-card suit.

(D) Pass. This hand contains only 12 points.

(E) Bid 1 Heart. This hand is worth 14 points (12 in high cards, 1 for the doubleton Spade, and 1 for the doubleton Club). A six-card suit is always biddable even if it does not contain an honor card.

(F) Bid 1 Heart. This hand is worth 14 points (12 in high cards and 2 for the singleton Spade). Since you have four-card suits, you start with the suit below the singleton.

(G) Bid 1 Diamond. This hand is worth 15 points (13 in high cards, 1 for the doubleton Heart, and 1 for the doubleton Club). Start with the five-card suit rather than the four-card suit.

(H) Bid 1 Club. This hand is worth 15 points (14 in high cards and 1 for the doubleton Diamond). You have two four-card suits and should start with the one below your doubleton.

(I) Bid 1 Spade. This hand is worth 15 points (12 in high cards, 2 for the singleton Club, and 1 for the doubleton Diamond). The proper opening with two five-card suits is the higher ranking suit (Spades), not the stronger suit (Hearts). With trump suits it is length rather than strength which concerns you.

The Two Demand Bid

The opening bid of two in a suit has a special meaning all its own. In a sense it may be considered an artificial bid. It is the strongest opening bid in Contract Bridge. The message which it conveys is something like this: "Partner, I have a hand of such great strength that I wish to reach a final game contract even if you have nothing. Since I am prepared for you to have nothing at all, I must have the necessary points in my own hand. It takes 26 points to make game, and I have at least 25 of them right here. Please keep bidding, however weak your hand may be, until we reach a game contract."

This opening two-bid is known as a forcing bid—a bid which forces partner to respond not only once, but at every opportunity, until a game contract is reached.

The requirements, generally speaking, are that opener should have in his own hand enough tricks to make all but one of the game-required tricks by himself. For example, to make an opening bid of 2 Spades, opener should be able to win nine tricks in his own hand. If the hand must be played in Diamonds, opener must be able to win ten tricks in his own hand to justify an opening 2 Diamond bid.

Here it is offered as a formula:

Requirements for Opening Two Demand Bid

(A) With a good five-card suit..................25 points
(B) With a good six-card suit...................23 points
(C) With a good seven-card suit.................21 points
 With a second good five-card suit: 1 point less than above.

EXAMPLES

(A)	(B)
♠ A K J x x	♠ A K Q J x x
♡ A	♡ A K x
◊ A K x	◊ A x
♣ K Q 10 x	♣ x x

(C)	(D)
♠ A K Q J x x x	♠ A Q x x x
♡ A x	♡ A K x
◇ x	◇ A K x
♣ A x x	♣ x x

(A) This hand is worth 26 points (24 in high cards and 2 points for the singleton).

(B) This hand contains 23 points (21 in high cards and 1 for each doubleton). With a good six-card suit 23 points are sufficient for a two demand bid.

(C) This hand contains 21 points (18 in high cards, 2 for the singleton, and 1 for the doubleton). With a good seven-card suit 21 points are sufficient for a two demand bid.

(D) This hand is worth only 21 points (20 in high cards and 1 for the doubleton), which, with a five-card suit, is not nearly enough for a two demand bid. It should be opened with 1 Spade.

Opening Pre-emptive Bids

This is a subject to which the beginner should give but scant attention. The use of an opening three-bid is not recommended to any but the most experienced players. Opening bids of three in a suit denote weak hands with a long suit. Their purpose is merely to annoy the opposition and compel them to start their bidding at a high level. Unseasoned players will frequently open with three of a suit with a good hand containing a long suit. This is improper. If such a hand contains 11 points in high cards, it is too good for an opening three-bid and must be opened with one of a suit.

Here is an example of a hand which might be opened with a bid of 3 Spades:

♠ K Q J x x x x   ♡ x x   ♢ x x   ♣ x x

Of course, this bid is made with the expectation of going down. But it may keep the opposition from getting together on a suit of their own.

Again we caution you against the too-frequent use of such a bid.

No Trump Bidding

I have preferred to take up the subject of No Trump bidding separately from suit bidding because there are basic differences between the two. In No Trump bidding it is not possible for an adversary to ruff away your Aces and Kings. High cards predominate, and we are not concerned with distribution points. In other words, no values are assigned to singletons and doubletons.

ACE	=	4 POINTS
KING	=	3 POINTS
QUEEN	=	2 POINTS
JACK	=	1 POINT

The entire pack contains 40 points

No Trump openings should be made only on hands which are more or less evenly divided. That is, your suits should be divided into one of the following patterns:

$$4\text{-}3\text{-}3\text{-}3$$
$$4\text{-}4\text{-}3\text{-}2$$
$$5\text{-}3\text{-}3\text{-}2$$

A 4-3-3-3 distribution means that you have four cards in one of your suits and three cards in each of the other three suits.

Example ♠ A Q x   ♡ K x x   ◊ Q J x   ♣ A J x x

A 4-4-3-2 distribution means that you have four cards in one of your suits, four cards in another suit, three cards in one suit, and two cards in the remaining suit.

Example ♠ A Q x   ♡ K x   ◊ Q J x x   ♣ A J x x

A 5-3-3-2 distribution means that you have five cards in one of your suits, 3 cards in each of two suits and two cards in your remaining suit.

Example ♠ A Q x   ♡ K x   ◊ Q J x   ♣ A J x x x

Observe that if you have a singleton (one-card suit), you must not open the bidding with 1 No Trump. If you have two doubletons (two-card suits), you must not open with 1 No Trump.

There are special high-card requirements for opening No Trump bids. Whereas you may open one of a suit with as little as 13 points (and some of those points may be for singletons and doubletons), your hand must contain a little more strength in high cards if you wish to open with 1 No Trump. The opening bid of 1 No Trump shows 16, 17, or 18 points. In No Trump bidding count only your high cards and do not allow a point for a doubleton. Of course, you will allow no credit for a singleton, because if you had a singleton you would not open with No Trump.

In order to qualify as an opening bid of 1 No Trump, your hand must meet another requirement. You must have PROTECTION in at least three of your suits. Now what is protection? Protection in this sense means that if the opponent who will have the opening lead against you has the rest of the high cards in a particular suit and leads them, you will eventually win at least one trick.

If you have the Ace, of course, you have the suit protected. If you have the King and one or more small cards with it, that is considered protection (or a STOPPER as it is more frequently referred to), because if the player who is on your left leads the Ace, your King will become high. If you have the Queen and two small cards, it is considered a stopper, because if your left-hand opponent leads the Ace and King, your Queen will become the high card. The same is true of the Jack when it is guarded by three small cards. If opponent leads the Ace, King, and Queen, the Jack becomes established, and will then take a trick.

Do not open with No Trump if your hand contains a worthless doubleton. That is to say, if you have a two-card suit it must include the Ace or King.

What about the size of the opening No Trump bid?

The opening 1 No Trump bid should contain 16-17-18 points.

The opening 2 No Trump bid should contain 22-23-24 points.

The opening 3 No Trump bid should contain 25-26-27 points.

What about hands containing 19-20-21 points? They belong in a special class. They are too big for 1 No Trump and not quite big enough for 2 No Trump; so they must be opened with one of a suit, and the full strength of the hand will be shown on the next round of the bidding.

Observe that when you open with 1 No Trump your hand may contain one unprotected suit (provided you have at least three cards in that suit). But when you open with 2 or 3 No Trump the requirements are stricter. All four suits must be protected.

The student should observe that:

26 points will normally produce 3 No Trump
33 points will normally produce 6 No Trump
37 points will normally produce 7 No Trump*

EXAMPLES

(A) ♠ Q J x   ♡ K J x   ◊ A Q x   ♣ K J x x
You have 17 points in high cards and a 4-3-3-3 distribution. This is a typical 1 No Trump opening bid.

(B) ♠ A Q x   ♡ x x x   ◊ A Q J x   ♣ K J x
You have only three suits stopped; but you have 17 points and a balanced hand. Therefore, the correct opening bid is 1 No Trump.

(C) ♠ x x x x   ♡ A x x   ◊ K x   ♣ A K x x
You have only 14 points. A No Trump bid requires 16 points; therefore, this hand should be opened with 1 Club.

(D) ♠ x x   ♡ A Q x   ◊ K J x   ♣ A Q x x x
This distribution falls into the No Trump category, and you have sufficient high-card points (16) to open with 1 No Trump. Nevertheless, you should not do so, because you have a worthless doubleton in Spades. Bid 1 Club.

(E) ♠ K x   ♡ A Q x   ◊ Q x x   ♣ A Q x x x
The best bid is 1 No Trump, which is superior to a bid of 1 Club. You hold 17 points in high cards.

---

* Since you have counted only high-card points, there cannot be an Ace (4 points) in opponents' hands.

(F) ♠ A J x   ♡ K Q x   ◇ A K J x   ♣ Q x x

This hand contains 20 points and is therefore too strong for a bid of 1 No Trump. You must open with 1 Diamond.

(G) ♠ Q 10 x   ♡ A K J   ◇ A K J x   ♣ A J x

This has the right distribution and 23 points, with all suits protected. It therefore fits the pattern and should be opened with 2 No Trump.

(H) ♠ A Q x   ♡ K Q 10 x x   ◇ K x   ♣ A K J

On this hand you should open with 2 No Trump. Your hand contains 22 points in high cards, with all suits protected.

(I) ♠ A K Q   ♡ A K J   ◇ Q 10 x   ♣ A Q J x

This balanced hand contains 26 points in high cards and should be opened with 3 No Trump.

CHAPTER V

RESPONSES TO OPENING BIDS

Keeping the Bidding Open

WHEN YOUR PARTNER opens the bidding with one of a suit and the next hand passes, a certain responsibility rests with you. If you pass and the other opponent passes, the bidding automatically ends. This may be a source of great disappointment to partner, who could conceivably have opened with a very strong hand and would like another chance to bid.

Obviously, you would not think of passing if you had a good hand. If you had as many as 13 points, you would naturally make some effort to get to a game contract; for with the knowledge that your partner, the opening bidder, has at least 13 points, you would realize that the partnership has the necessary 26 points. However, in many cases you will have less than 13 points, and yet you must not abandon hope for game, because partner might have opened with considerably more than 13 points. An opening bid of one in a suit will sometimes be made on 20, 21, or 22 points. Remember that if partner (the opener) has 20, you will need only 6 to produce game.

The question therefore arises: "What is the least number of points I should have in order to keep the bidding open for partner *and give him another chance to bid?*"

Whenever your partner has made an opening bid and the next

player has passed, you should try to keep the bidding open (by making some bid) if you have at least 6 points in your hand. For this purpose, you may calculate both high cards and distribution. In other words, if you can keep the bidding open without increasing the contract (that is, at the level of one), you may do so with 5 points in high cards if you have at least 1 point for a doubleton.

With hands of moderate strength (about 6 to 9 points), you may keep the bidding open in one of three ways:

(A) By bidding 1 No Trump

(B) By bidding one of another suit

(C) By raising your partner from one to two of his suit

(A) *By bidding 1 No Trump*

What should you do when you have strength enough to respond but neither adequate trump support (four small trumps or three trumps headed by Queen or better) nor a biddable suit of your own. You should bid 1 No Trump.

If your partner has bid one of a suit, and you have at least 6 points, you may show your suit if you can do so at the level of one; but if you are unable to bid a suit at the level of one, because it is a lower-ranking suit, you should bid 1 No Trump to keep the bidding open. Such a response advises that you have 6 to 9 points in high cards (remember that in bidding No Trump you do not count values for singletons and doubletons but only the high-card content of the hand). The response of 1 No Trump differs from the response in a new suit in this respect: that the opening bidder need not speak again. He may pass if he chooses.*

---

* Let us remind you that if you open with one of a suit and your partner in response names a new suit, you are obliged to bid once more. A new suit by responder is a one-round force; but if responder gives you a single raise in your suit, or bids 1 No Trump, you need not bid again.

If you have greater strength than this, you must take a different form of action, which will be discussed in the section on responding with good hands.

Examples of responses of 1 No Trump:

Your partner opens with 1 Spade. You hold:

   ♠ x x   ♡ x x x   ♢ K x x   ♣ K J x x x

Respond 1 No Trump. You have 7 points in high cards. The hand is not strong enough to increase the contract to 2 Clubs.

   ♠ x x x   ♡ Q x x   ♢ K x x   ♣ A x x x

Respond 1 No Trump. You have 9 points, a maximum, and no biddable suit at the one level.

   ♠ x x x   ♡ K x x   ♢ K x x   ♣ x x x x

Respond 1 No Trump. You have 6 points, a minimum.

   ♠ x x x   ♡ K x x   ♢ x x x   ♣ Q x x x

Pass. You have only 5 points.

(B) *By bidding one of another suit*

If you have a biddable suit and a hand worth at least 6 points (including high cards and distribution), you may show that suit if you can do so by bidding only one in the suit.

For example:

Your partner opens with 1 Heart, and you hold:

   ♠ K x x x x   ♡ x x   ♢ x x x   ♣ Q x x

Respond 1 Spade. Since you are making a suit response, this hand is worth 6 points (5 in high cards and 1 for the doubleton).

Let us change the illustration slightly:

♠ Q x x   ♥ x x   ♦ x x x   ♣ K x x x x

Again your partner opens with 1 Heart, and the next hand passes. What should you do? You should pass. There is no suit which you can bid at the level of one; and if you choose to keep the bidding open with 1 No Trump, you need 6 points in high cards. You have only 5 points. (When bidding No Trump we do not count doubletons.)

(C) *Raising your partner*

If you have support for partner's trump suit, you may give a single raise—that is, 1 Spade to 2 Spades, or 1 Heart to 2 Hearts if your hand contains 6 to 10 points (not less than 6; not more than 10).

When your partner opens the bidding with one of a suit, the first question you will have to decide is whether you are satisfied with partner's suit as trump; for if you are not satisfied, you will try to find a better trump. In order to be satisfied with partner's suit, you must have adequate trump support. Adequate trump support consists of:

x x x x
A x x
K x x
Q x x
J 10 x

If you do not have this much strength in partner's suit, you will wish to make some bid other than a raise of partner's suit.

In valuing your hand as a dummy (in support of partner's suit), you add the value of your high cards to the values for your short suits. But the short-suit values differ when you are the dummy hand. If you are bidding your own suit, it will be remembered that you count:

> 1 point for a doubleton
> 2 points for a singleton
> 3 points for a void

But when you are raising partner's suit, you count:
> "Dummy Points"*

> 1 point for a doubleton
> 3 points for a singleton
> 5 points for a void

For example:
Partner opens with 1 Heart, and you hold:

	(A)		(B)
♠	x x	♠	x
♡	A x x x	♡	A x x x
◇	Q x x x	◇	Q x x x
♣	x x x	♣	K x x x

(A) This hand qualifies as a raise of your partner's bid from 1 Heart to 2 Hearts. First of all, you have adequate trump support; secondly, you have 7 points in support of Hearts, 6 in high cards and 1 for the doubleton Spade.

(B) This hand contains adequate trump support and is worth 12 points in support of Hearts, 9 points in high cards and 3 for the singleton Spade. (Note that a singleton counts 3 points when you are raising partner.) Since the hand is worth 12 points, it is

---

* As you gain in experience it will be pointed out to you that certain deductions must be made if the dummy contains only three trumps instead of four, but at the present stage of your development we deem it better to skip over this point. You will also subsequently learn of the promoted values of high cards in your partner's suit, but for the present you must value the cards in your partner's suit the same as any other high cards.

too strong for a raise to 2 Hearts and must be treated differently. (A response of 2 Clubs is made; and when this player gets his next turn to bid, he will raise the Hearts.) This subject will be discussed at a later stage. (See page 65.)

Responding with Strong Hands

Before proceeding with this subject it is well to take a few moments to study the general meaning of some of the more common bids.

One of the basic principles of Contract Bridge is that when opener starts with one of a suit and responder names any new suit, the opener must bid once more. This is known as the NEW SUIT FORCING PRINCIPLE.

For example:

	Opener	*Responder*
(1)	1 Heart	1 Spade

	Opener	*Responder*
(2)	1 Spade	2 Diamonds

In each of these cases opener must make another bid, even though he opened with a minimum hand.

If responder gives opener a single raise in his own suit, opener need not bid again if he does not choose to do so. Thus:

Opener	*Responder*
1 Spade	2 Spades

Opener may pass. Similarly, if responder replies with 1 No Trump. That is not a new suit, and opener may pass.

For example:

Opener	Responder
1 Spade	1 No Trump

Opener may pass.

When responder jumps the bid, either in his own suit, in partner's suit, or in No Trump, he shows a strong hand, and the opener must keep on bidding until game is reached. Jump bids by responder are forcing to game.

For example:

Opener	Responder
1 Spade	3 Spades

Opener is forced to bid, and game must be reached.

Opener	Responder
1 Spade	3 Hearts

Opener is forced to bid, and game must be reached.

Opener	Responder
1 Spade	2 No Trump

Opener is forced to bid, and game must be reached, i.e., partners must keep on bidding until game contract is reached.

The next important consideration in responding is to value your hand in order to decide whether or not your side probably can make game. The best way to judge is this: It takes 26 points to produce game, and when your partner opens with one of a suit, you are to presume that he has at least 13 points. If you have 13 or more, you should make a distinct effort to reach game.

In the preceding section we have discussed keeping the bidding open with weak hands. In the ensuing pages I shall try to suggest to you how to respond with strong hands.

(A) *Jump raise in the same suit* (1 Spade—3 Spades). This bid is forcing to game.

(B) *Jump take-out in No Trump* (1 Spade—2 No Trump). This bid is forcing to game.

(C) *Jump in a new suit* (1 Spade—3 Diamonds, or 1 Heart—2 Spades). This bid is forcing to game and suggests that the partnership may have as many as 33 points and, therefore, possibly a slam. It shows at least 19 points in the responder's hand.

(D) *Take-out into one of a new suit* (1 Club—1 Heart). This bid is ambiguous. It may be a hand as weak as 6 points, and it may be a hand as strong as 18 points, but responder will make it clear on the next round.

(E) *Take-out into two of a new suit* (1 Heart—2 Diamonds). This bid increases the contract and is therefore encouraging. It is forcing for one round. It shows at least 10 points and may be as many as 18.

(A) *Jump raise in the same suit*

Your partner has opened the bidding with 1 Heart, and you hold:

♠ x   ♡ A x x x   ◊ K Q x x   ♣ J 10 x x

You have adequate trump support for Hearts, and your hand as a dummy for Hearts is worth 13 points, 10 points in high cards and 3 for the singleton Spade. (Remember a singleton in the dummy is worth 3 points, whereas it is worth only 2 points in the hand of the person bidding his own suit.)

You know that your partner has at least 13 points, and you have 13. This produces a total of 26, and you wish to contract for game. How do you announce yourself to partner? By making a jump bid: that is, bidding one more than you have to. In other words, bid 3 Hearts. This jump, which is known as a DOUBLE RAISE, forces opener to bid again, and you must reach game.

You may ask, "If you know that the partnership has 26 points and you wish to reach a game in Hearts, why won't you just bid 4 Hearts?" That is a good question. The answer is that the double jump, that is, 1 Heart—4 Hearts, instead of the simple jump of 1 Heart—3 Hearts, has a special meaning which need not concern you here.

In order to jump from one to three of your partner's suit you should have not merely adequate trump support, but you should have at least four of your partner's trumps and a point count of 13, 14, 15 or 16, including high cards and distribution.

Observe the hand shown above. Your partner has opened with 1 Heart. You have 4 Hearts headed by the Ace (this is more than adequate trump support). You have 10 points in high cards and your singleton Spade is worth 3 points, when you are supporting partner. Your hand is therefore worth 13 points and, since opener is expected to have 13 points, you have the necessary 26 for game. You demand a game by jumping to 3 Hearts and partner must go on to game.

(B) *Jump take-out in No Trump*

Your partner has opened the bidding with 1 Spade, and you hold:

♠ J x   ♡ K x x x   ◊ K J x   ♣ A J x x

You have 13 points in high cards, the equal of an opening bid. Your partner is presumed to have 13, so you apparently have the 26 points required for game. In what contract would you like to reach game? You have not adequate trump support for Spades, and you have no very good suit of your own. But you have protection (stoppers)* in the other three suits, and you would like to play the hand at a final contract of 3 No Trump. How do you transmit this message to partner? By making a jump to 2 No Trump. This forces partner to bid until a game contract is reached, because under our conventions when the responder makes a jump response, it is mandatory for his side to reach a game contract. Again you may ask why not bid 3 No Trump yourself. The answer is that the 2 No Trump response affords the opening bidder a cheap chance to show another suit if he has one; and, furthermore, a jump to 3 No Trump is a special bid which promises more high cards than a jump to 2 No Trump.

The 2 No Trump response shows an evenly balanced hand with 13, 14, or 15 points.

The 3 No Trump response is used to show a hand which contains 16, 17, or 18 points.

Your partner opens with 1 Spade. You hold:

(1) ♠ x x x   ♡ Q 10 x   ◇ K J x x   ♣ A K x

(2) ♠ 10 x   ♡ A Q 10   ◇ K x x x x   ♣ K Q x

(3) ♠ J x x   ♡ A Q x   ◇ K J x x   ♣ A Q x

(1) Bid 2 No Trump, forcing to game. You have 13 points with all unbid suits protected.

(2) Bid 2 No Trump, forcing to game. You have 14 points with all unbid suits protected.

---

* A stopper means that, if the opponent who will have the opening lead against you has the rest of the high cards in a particular suit and leads them, you will eventually win at least one trick.

(3) Bid 3 No Trump. You have 17 points, a 4-3-3-3 distribution, and all suits protected.

(C) *Jump in a new suit* (1 Spade—3 Diamonds; or 1 Heart —2 Spades)

Your partner opens the bidding with 1 Heart, and you hold:

♠ x   ♡ K J x x   ◇ A K J x x   ♣ A x x

In support of Hearts your hand is worth 19 points. You know that your partner's hand is worth at least 13, which gives the partnership a total of at least 32 points and places you on the verge of a slam. If partner has even a single extra point, you will have enough for a slam in Hearts. How do you flash the signal? By bidding one more than necessary in a new suit, 3 Diamonds. This is known as a JUMP SHIFT and announces that you surely have game and are interested in a slam.

Note that if you wished to make a simple take-out in Diamonds, it would be necessary to bid only 2 Diamonds. When you bid 3 Diamonds, which is exactly one more than is necessary, it is a jump shift.

(D) *Take-out into one of a new suit*

This bid covers a wide range of hands. It may be made on a hand which contains only 6 points, and it may also be made on a hand which is worth 18 points. (If it were worth more than 18 you would make a jump shift.)

For example:

Partner opens with 1 Heart. You hold:

(1) ♠ K x x x x   ♡ x x   ◇ Q x x   ♣ x x x

(2) ♠ A K x x x   ♡ A 10 x x   ◇ x   ♣ A x x

(1) This is worth 6 points (5 in high cards and 1 for the doubleton). You therefore keep the bidding open by bidding 1 Spade. But you do not expect to bid any more.

(2) This hand is worth 18 dummy points in support of Hearts, (15 in high cards and 3 for the singleton) not quite strong enough for a jump shift. So you bid 1 Spade as a temporizing measure. There is no danger of failing to reach game, because when you mention a new suit your partner, the opener, must bid again, and you may act more vigorously on the next round.

(E) *Take-out into two of a new suit*

When your partner opens the bidding with one of a suit, you may respond with one of some other suit with as little as 6 points. But, if in order to show your own suit you must bid two of that suit, you will need considerably more strength. You are then required to have at least 10 points.

For example:

Partner opens with 1 Club. You hold:

♠ A x x   ♡ x x   ◊ K 10 x x x   ♣ x x x

Your response is 1 Diamond. Your hand is worth 8 points (7 in high cards and 1 for the doubleton).

But if your partner had opened the bidding with 1 Heart (instead of 1 Club), you would have had a more difficult problem in responding. "Shall I show my Diamonds?" you might ask. The answer: In order to do so you would have had to bid 2 Diamonds. In order to respond with two of a new suit you need a good hand (at least 10 points) and here your hand is not good enough. It is worth only 8 points. Obviously you may not pass because when your partner opens the bidding you must make some response if you have 6 or more points. But with this indifferent hand, you must make your response at the level of one. The only response that you can make at the level of one is 1 No Trump, which shows 6, 7, 8, or 9 points in high cards.

If your hand were a little stronger:

♠ A x x　　♡ x x　　♢ K Q J x x　　♣ x x x

Now, if partner opened with 1 Heart, you could properly bid 2 Diamonds. Your hand is worth 11 points (10 in high cards and 1 for the doubleton).

Responses to Two Demand Bid

When partner makes an opening bid of two in a suit and you have a very weak hand, you make the technical response of 2 No Trump. This is really an artificial bid which says, "Partner, I have very little, if any, high-card strength, and I wish to discourage you. My 2 No Trump bid does not mean that I desire to play the hand at No Trump."

The 2 No Trump response is sometimes called the BUST RESPONSE, though it does not necessarily mean that the responder has a complete blank. He may have a little something but not enough to make what we call a POSITIVE RESPONSE.

In order to make a positive response, responder's hand must be worth at least 7 points. So, if he has a suit of his own with less than 7 points, he must not show it on the first round. He must first make the negative response of 2 No Trump and then show his suit on the next round if he chooses to.

For example:

Partner opens with 2 Hearts, and you hold:

♠ x x x   ♡ x x   ◊ 10 x x x   ♣ x x x x

You may not pass. An opening bid of two in a suit demands that partners keep bidding until game is reached. Bid 2 No Trump.

♠ x x x x   ♡ x x   ◊ K x x x   ♣ Q x x

Respond 2 No Trump. You have only 5 points.

♠ A x x x   ♡ x x x   ◊ x x x   ♣ x x x

Respond 2 No Trump. You have only 4 points.

♠ Q J 9 x x x   ♡ x x   ◊ x x x   ♣ x x

Respond 2 No Trump, not 2 Spades. You have not enough strength for a positive response, which requires at least 7 points. If partner rebids 3 Hearts, you should then bid 3 Spades. Partner will realize then that you have a fairly good Spade suit but not much high card strength.

♠ x   ♡ Q x x x x   ◊ x x x   ♣ x x x x

Respond 2 No Trump, even though you have good support for Hearts, for you lack the necessary points (7 points for a positive response). But on the next round you should raise Hearts.

If your hand is worth 7 points, or more, you make a natural, or positive, response.

For example:

Your partner opens with 2 Hearts. You hold:

♠ K 10 x x x   ♡ x x   ◊ x x x   ♣ A x x

Your response is 2 Spades. You have 7 points in high cards, and, valued at Spades, you have an additional point for distribution (the doubleton Heart).

In order to show your own suit in response to partner's two demand bid, the suit should be at least five cards long and be headed by at least 3 points (King or Queen-Jack).

When you hold a fairly good hand, without support for partner and without a good suit of your own, you may respond with 3 No Trump. Such a response will show about 7 or 8 points in high cards.

Responses to No Trump Bids

In replying to partner's No Trump bids, it is important to bear in mind that 26 points will normally produce game. The responder adds his points to those expected from partner, and in many cases he can tell at once exactly how many the partnership possesses.

If the responder has a normal type of hand with only 7 high-card points, he knows that the partnership will not have game; for even if partner has 18 points, his 7 will bring the total to only 25, just short of the necessary 26. Since there is no game, there is nothing to be gained by bidding, and responder should pass and permit the opener to play at 1 No Trump.

On the other hand, responder may have 10 points in high cards. In that case, he knows that there is game in the hand, because he is assured that the partnership has 26 points. Remember that the opener has at least 16 points, which, added to his 10, yields the necessary total. Therefore, responder bids 3 No Trump.

But responder may have 8 or 9 points, in which case he cannot be sure that his side has game, for if partner has only 16 points, they will not have the necessary 26. But if partner has a little more than 16, they may have. Responder therefore raises to 2 No Trump. This requests the opener to go on to three if he opened with more than just 16 points.

When responder has a long suit and less than 7 points in high cards, he may not raise to 2 No Trump; but he may feel that it would be safer to play the hand at two of his suit rather than 1 No Trump. When responder bids 2 Clubs or 2 Diamonds, opener should take it as a warning and should not go on. For example, partner opens with 1 No Trump, and you hold:

♠ x   ♥ x x   ♦ Q 10 x x x x   ♣ K x x x

You should bid 2 Diamonds, which partner should permit you to play.

But if you held:

♠ x x   ♥ x x x   ♦ Q 10 x x x   ♣ K x x

You should not bid 2 Diamonds. You have what is known as an evenly balanced hand and have no objection to partner's playing at 1 No Trump. Having only 5 high-card points, you pass.

If you have a very long suit in Hearts or Spades and also enough points to make you feel that you have game (10 points or more: 16+10=26), you should make a JUMP BID in your suit—that is:

<blockquote>
1 No Trump   3 Spades
</blockquote>
or
<blockquote>
1 No Trump   3 Hearts
</blockquote>

For example: Your partner opens with 1 No Trump. You hold:

♠ K Q J x x x   ♥ A x x   ♦ x x   ♣ x x

You have 10 points in high cards and therefore enough to justify a raise to 3 No Trump, but you have an unbalanced hand with a six-card Spade suit and might prefer to play the hand in Spades (at Spades your hand is worth 12 points, 10 in high cards and 2 for distribution). Your proper response is, therefore, 3

Spades—a jump take-out. A jump in a suit after an opening No Trump bid does not necessarily suggest a slam.

EXAMPLES

Your partner opens with 1 No Trump. You hold:

(a) ♠ Q x   ♥ J x x   ♦ K x x x x   ♣ x x x

Pass. You have only 6 points and a balanced hand.

(b) ♠ x x x   ♥ A Q x x x   ♦ J x   ♣ Q x x

Your hand is balanced and contains 9 points in high cards and a five-card suit. Raise to 2 No Trump. This is better than bidding 2 Hearts.

(c) ♠ x x   ♥ K x x   ♦ A 10 9 x x   ♣ J x x

Don't bid 2 Diamonds. You have 8 points in high cards, sufficient to bid 2 No Trump. (A raise to 2 No Trump may be given with only 7 points if you have a fairly good five-card suit.)

(d) ♠ Q x   ♥ Q J x x   ♦ A x x   ♣ K J x x

You have 13 points. Partner has between 16 and 18. If he has 16, the combined total will be 29 points. If he has 18, the combined total will be 31 points. Therefore, you cannot possibly reach the 33 points necessary for a slam, but more than 26 points are held by the two hands. Bid 3 No Trump.

(e) ♠ J x x x   ♥ Q x x   ♦ A x x   ♣ K x x

Your point count is 10. Partner has at least 16. The total reaches the necessary 26 points. Bid 3 No Trump.

(f) ♠ A 10 x   ♥ K J x   ♦ A x x x   ♣ K Q x

You have 17 points. Partner is known to have a minimum of 16; so the partnership is blessed with a total of at least 33 points. Bid 6 No Trump. Note that you need not fear missing a good contract of 7 No Trump. If partner has the maximum of 18, the combined total will only reach 35 points and still be short of the required 37.

Responses to Opening Bid of 2 No Trump

When your partner opens with 2 No Trump, you know that he has at least 22 points. If you have 4 points and an evenly balanced hand, you should raise to 3 No Trump, for you know that the partnership has at least 26 points.

If you have 9 or more points in support of an opening 2 No Trump bid, there may be slam possibilities, which we will discuss in the chapter on slam bidding. (See page 93.)

If responder has 4 points and a good five-card suit in Spades or Hearts, he should bid three of that suit, and the opening bidder may decide whether to return to 3 No Trump or bid four of his partner's suit.

Partner opens with 2 No Trump. You hold:

(A) ♠ x x x   ♡ A x x   ◇ K x x   ♣ J x x x

Bid 3 No Trump. You have 8 points.

(B) ♠ x x x   ♡ Q x x   ◇ J x x   ♣ x x x x

Pass. You have only 3 points, and 4 points are required for a raise from 2 No Trump to 3 No Trump.

(C) ♠ x x x   ♡ x x x   ◇ x x x   ♣ K J x x

Bid 3 No Trump. You have 4 points.

(D) ♠ K 10 x x x   ♡ Q x x   ◇ x   ♣ x x x x

Bid 3 Spades. You have a five-card major suit and 5 points in high cards.

(E) ♠ A x x   ♡ K x x x   ◇ Q x x   ♣ K x x

Bid 6 No Trump. Partner has at least 22 points and you have 12, so you have the necessary points. (See page 94.)

Responses to Opening Bid of 3 No Trump

When partner opens with 3 No Trump, you know that he has 25, 26, or 27 points, and you also have no further concern about getting to game. However, you should be interested in the figures 33 or 34, for if you discover that the partnership has that many points you will wish to bid for a small slam. If you have 9 points, you may add that to partner's 25 and reach the total of 34. You should therefore bid 6 No Trump. If you have a little less than 9, there may or may not be a slam, but the management of situations of this character will be taken up in the chapter on slam bidding. (See page 93.)

CHAPTER VI

REBIDS BY OPENING BIDDER

THE FIRST BID made at the table is the OPENING BID. The first
bid made by his partner is a RESPONSE. When the opener or
responder bids on his subsequent turn, it is called a REBID, and
the rebid is one of the most important calls in the auction.

The opening bid is usually quite indefinite. If it is one of a
suit, it may be as little as 13 points and as many as 21 or 23.
Similarly with the response; that, too, may be rather indefinite.
When it is made at the level of one (of a new suit), it may be
as little as 6 points and as many as 18. If the response was made
at the level of two (of a new suit), it may be as little as 10 and
as many as 18.

On your rebid you usually try to narrow down the range of
your strength and tell your partner into what bracket your hand
falls. Some rebids will show that your hand is in the minimum
range (13-14-15). Some rebids will show that your hand was
above minimum range and that you had considerable additional
values (16-17-18). Some rebids will show that you have a great
deal of additional values, in which case you jump the bid (19-
20). Some rebids show that you absolutely insist upon game
(21-22).

How to Indicate a Minimum Rebid

There are several ways in which opening bidder may indicate
a minimum bid, if partner has responded with one of a suit.

Presume the bidding has gone:

Opener	*Responder*
1 Diamond	1 Heart
?	

(A) *By rebidding his own suit.* If opener rebids 2 Diamonds, he shows a hand containing a rebiddable Diamond suit but probably only 13, 14, or 15 points.

Example:

♠ x x   ♡ x x   ♢ A K J x x   ♣ A x x x

Opener's rebid of 2 Diamonds announces, "Partner, I have a good five-card Diamond suit (rebiddable), but I have a hand of the minimum class, that is, 13, 14, or 15 points."

(B) *By rebidding 1 No Trump.* If opener rebids 1 No Trump, it shows an evenly divided hand with 13, 14, or 15 points.

Example:

♠ K x x   ♡ x x x   ♢ A Q J x   ♣ A x x

Opener's rebid of 1 No Trump announces, "Partner, I have an evenly divided hand, in the minimum range. That is, I have 13, 14, or 15 points. I have no special support for your Hearts; I have not another suit which I wish to show you."

(C) *Opener may rebid in another suit at the level of one without showing additional values.* If opener rebids 1 Spade, it does not promise any more than a minimum.

Example:

♠ A Q x x   ♡ x x   ♢ A K x x   ♣ x x x

Remember you opened with 1 Diamond and partner responded 1 Heart. You then chose to rebid 1 Spade. This bid did not necessarily show any additional values. The rebid at the level of one may be made even if opener has only 13 points. In this case, you as opener have 14 points.

(D) *Opener may show a hand of minimum rank* (13-14-15) *by raising responder's suit from one to two.*

For example:

♠ A 10 x x   ♡ x x   ◇ A K J x   ♣ J 10 x

Opener	Responder
1 Diamond	1 Spade
2 Spades	

You opened with 1 Diamond and partner responded 1 Spade. Your bid of 2 Spades announces, "Partner, don't get too excited. I haven't very much more than a minimum hand. I have some trump support for you, at least 3 headed by an honor, but don't count on me for more than 14 or 15 points."

How to Indicate More Than a Minimum Rebid

(A) *By bidding a new suit at the level of three.*

For example:

♠ x   ♡ K Q 10 9 x   ◇ K x   ♣ A K J x x

Opener	Responder
1 Heart	2 Diamonds
3 Clubs	

This shows a strong hand.

(B) *By giving responder a double raise.*

For example:

♠ A 10 x x   ♡ K J x x   ◇ x   ♣ A K x x

Opener	Responder
1 Club	1 Spade
3 Spades	

This hand is worth 18 points in support of Spades, and opener shows a strong hand by giving a double raise.

(C) *Opener may show a strong hand* (19 points) *by jumping the bid on the second round.*

For example:

♠ Q x ♡ K J x ◇ A K J x ♣ A J x x

Opener	Responder
1 Diamond	1 Spade
2 No Trump	

Opener's hand contains 19 points and all suits are protected, which he shows by jumping to 2 No Trump. If responder has about 7 points, the partnership will have the 26 points necessary for game.

Preference Bids

When your partner has bid two suits, it is important for you to choose for trump that suit which is best for the combined hands, without regard to which suit a particular player personally prefers. In expressing a preference, remember that in numbers there is strength. Pick the suit in which the partnership has the most trumps, not necessarily the higher trumps.

A preference for one of partner's two suits may be expressed in one of two ways: (a) by passing if you prefer his second suit; (b) by returning to his first suit if that is the one which is better for the partnership.

For example:

Your partner has bid Spades and then Hearts, and you hold:

♠ 4 3 2 ♡ A K ◇ J x x x ♣ 10 x x x

Your partner opens with 1 Spade and you respond 1 No Trump (you have 8 points); your partner rebids 2 Hearts. If you prefer Hearts you may pass, but actually your preference should be for Spades and you should return to 2 Spades. This is not a raise. It is merely a return to your partner's first suit.

Let us assume that your partner has five Spades and five Hearts. If you choose Hearts as trumps, your partnership will have a total of only seven trumps against six for the opponents. Whereas, if you select Spades for trumps, your side will have eight Spades against five for the opposition.

When you hold the same number of cards in each of partner's suits, it is usually good practice to return to his first suit, for there is a better chance that his first suit will be longer.

Partner	You
(Opener)	(Responder)
1 Spade	1 No Trump
2 Hearts	

You have:

♠ x x x　　♡ x x　　♢ K x x x　　♣ K x x x

It is your duty to return to 2 Spades because you prefer that suit. You must not argue, "I have only 6 points and have already showed it by my 1 No Trump bid. I cannot bid any more." It is always your duty to see that the hand is played in the best partnership trump, and your return to 2 Spades is not really a bid in the true sense of the word.

Another example:

Partner	You
1 Heart	1 No Trump
2 Spades	

You have:

♠ x x　　♡ J x x　　♢ K x x x　　♣ K x x x

What should you bid now? 3 Hearts, even though it involves increasing the contract. This is not really a raise. It is your solemn duty to return to the suit in which the partnership has more trumps. You know that your partner has five Hearts and four Spades. (If he had the same number of each he would have bid Spades, the higher ranking suit, first.) The partnership, therefore, has eight Hearts as against only six Spades. It would be folly to pass his 2 Spade bid.

CHAPTER VII

DEFENSIVE BIDDING

Up until this point we have limited our discussions to those hands on which we have been bidding against silent opponents. But in real life we find that interference from the opposition is more often than not to be encountered. The auction is an open function, and anyone may bid who is willing to take the risk. If an opponent opens the bidding, you are at perfect liberty to insert a bid of your own. The side which has not opened the bidding is known as the DEFENSIVE TEAM. A bid which is made by one of the defenders is known as an OVERCALL.

For example:

South opens with 1 Heart. West holds:

♠ A K J x x   ♥ x x   ♦ K x x   ♣ x x x

He decides to put in a bid of 1 Spade. This bid is known as an overcall, or defensive bid. Defensive bids are much more risky than opening bids. The overcaller knows that one of his opponents (the opener) has a good hand, which makes it more probable that partner of the overcaller will have very little strength. There is a further deterrent to making questionable overcalls. The person who opens the bidding has hopes of reaching a game contract and reaping the bonus that goes with it. He is therefore justified in taking some risk of going down by bidding. But, when one adversary has already shown strength, the chances of a defender making a game are considerably reduced; and it is not good policy to take needless risks, for the opponents have the privilege of doubling you.

When contemplating an overcall, it is good policy to count up in businesslike fashion the number of tricks you fully expect to win. Bear in mind the number of tricks for which you are contracting and determine how far you are from your goal. This will reveal to you how great a risk you are taking. It is no disgrace to be set 500 points in an overcall; so you have a leeway of three tricks if you are not vulnerable and two tricks if you are vulnerable.

In other words, if your right-hand opponent has opened the bidding with 1 Spade, for example, and you contemplate bidding two of some suit, you ought to be able to win in your own hand six of the eight tricks for which you are contracting (if you are vulnerable). In other words, if you are doubled by the enemy, you will go down no more than two tricks which would be 500 points. If you are not vulnerable, you may take slightly greater liberties and may overcall with two of a suit, even if you can win only five tricks, for then if you are doubled you will go down no more than three tricks, which is still a 500-point loss.

When you overcall at the level of two, be sure you have a good trump suit; and do not be too much concerned with your point count. Do not overcall at the two level with suits like this:

A Q 6 4 2
(or) K J 7 5 3
(or) Q 10 6 5 2

for if the player sitting to your left has the remaining trumps, you may lose three or four tricks in trumps alone.

These look more like the proper trump suits with which to overcall:

A K J 9 4

(or) K Q J 9 7

(or) Q J 10 9 6 3

In other words, don't overcall at the level of two with any suit in which you might lose more than two tricks in the trump suit itself.

For example:
An opponent opens the bidding with 1 Spade, and you hold:

Hand A	*Hand B*
♠ 6 3	♠ 6 3 2
♡ K Q J 9 8 5	♡ K J 7 6 4
◊ A 7 5	◊ A 4
♣ 9 2	♣ A 8 2

With Hand A, bid 2 Hearts. This is a good solid trump suit, and there is little or no risk of disaster. Note that this hand contains only 10 points in high cards but it can win 6 tricks, five in Hearts and one in Diamonds.

With Hand B, do not overcall with 2 Hearts. Even though this hand contains 12 points in high cards it does not offer safety. Your trump suit is of such character that you might lose three or four trump tricks if you run into a vicious left-hand opponent who has the missing Heart honors. You might win only four tricks with this hand.

Responding to Partner's Overcall

When your partner makes an overcall, do not treat it as an opening bid; therefore you must not keep the bidding open for him unless you have a good hand. No more take-outs or raises with 6 points. You do not bid in this situation unless you have almost the equal of an opening bid yourself—that is, about 11 points in high cards.

For example:
Your left-hand opponent opens with 1 Heart. Your partner overcalls with 1 Spade. You hold:

♠ x x   ♡ x x x   ◇ A Q x x x   ♣ K x x

Don't bid 2 Diamonds. If partner had opened, you would keep the bidding alive. But since he has made a mere overcall, you pass.

If your partner has made an overcall in a suit which pleases you highly, and you think that your partnership may have at least 26 points, you should make an effort to reach game. How is this done? Let us take an illustration. You, as South, hold:

♠ K J x   ♡ x   ◇ A Q 10 x x   ♣ x x x x

If your partner (North) had opened with 1 Spade, you would respond with 2 Diamonds. You would not be concerned lest partner pass because when he opened with one of a suit and you named a new suit, he was obligated to bid again, so you were sure to get a chance to help Spades on the next round. You did not respond with a mere raise to 2 Spades because your hand was too good for a single raise.

But if West had opened the bidding with 1 Heart and your partner had overcalled with 1 Spade, you would be faced with a different problem. If you decided to bid 2 Diamonds, you might not get another chance. Your mentioning a new suit does not force partner to bid again because he is *not the opening bidder*. You should therefore raise to 2 Spades, which says, "Partner, I am not just keeping the bidding open, because we are not expected to keep open a mere overcall; but I have about 12 points, and if you have a rather good overcall, we may have enough for game."

Though most overcalls are made in a suit, occasionally an overcall may be made in No Trump.

For example:

East, your right-hand opponent, has opened the bidding with 1 Diamond, and you (South) hold:

    ♠ K 10 x   ♡ A J x   ◇ K Q x   ♣ A 10 x x

You may overcall with 1 No Trump. This bid describes a hand which is evenly divided, has good protection in the opponents' suit, and has the count for an ordinary opening bid of 1 No Trump—that is 16, 17, or 18 points. In other words, an overcall of 1 No Trump is made on the same type of hand as an original opening 1 No Trump bid.

The Take-out Double

When an adversary has made a bid and undertaken to win a certain number of tricks, and you think you can prevent him from winning that number of tricks, you may call "double" (which doubles the amount of the penalty he may sustain for going down). This is called a PENALTY DOUBLE.

But there is another type of double, known as the TAKE-OUT DOUBLE. This serves as a signal to your partner. When the double is used in this manner, it is not with the expectation that you will defeat the contract. It serves as a message to partner that you wish him to bid his best suit (however weak it may be) so that the hand will be played by your side rather than by your opponents.

But the question will be raised: "When my partner doubles, how will I know whether he means it for a penalty double or for a take-out double?" This will be demonstrated presently.

When an opponent has opened the bidding against you, the chances are against your scoring a game on that deal. Nevertheless it is proper for you to put up a fight of some kind by over-calling, in an attempt to play the hand yourself at some low contract.

In order to make such an overcall it is not required that you have the same high-card strength as the opening bidder. However, occasionally, after an opponent has opened the bidding, you will find yourself in possession of a strong hand, perhaps as good as or even better than an opening bid. You may acquaint your partner with this fact by means of a take-out double. If your opponent opens with one of a suit, and you are second hand and you double, that is a signal for your partner to bid. But if you double *after* your partner has already made a bid, that is not for a take-out, but for penalties.

For example:

You are South. The bidding has proceeded:

North	East	South
1 Heart	1 Spade	Double

This double is for penalties. It could not mean: "Partner, I wish you to bid your best suit," because North presumably has already done so. It therefore means: "I double because I think I can defeat a contract of 1 Spade."

However, if the bidding has proceeded:

North	East	South
Pass	1 Diamond	Double

This double is for partner to take out. It announces: "Partner, you have not yet bid (remember that a pass is not considered to be a bid), and I wish to force you to bid your best suit."

Similarly:

West	North	East	South
1 Heart	Pass	2 Hearts	Double

This double is for a take-out. It means to say: "Partner, you have not yet bid, and even though the auction is up to the level of two, it is my first chance to assert myself, and I insist upon hearing from you."

When your partner makes a take-out double it is an absolute command. You MUST bid. Under no circumstances may you refuse to do so, however weak your hand may be. (There is an exception: when you hold extreme length or strength in the opponents' suit.) Even if you have no face card, you must name your best suit, though it happens to be no better than 5-4-3-2.

Obviously, therefore, doubler should have a good hand and be prepared to avoid disaster if you happen to have a blank hand.

What Strength Should Take-out Doubler Have?

In order to make a take-out double, a player should have a hand which is at least as good as an opening bid, preferably a little better. The absolute minimum, therefore, would be 13 points if a suit has been bid, or 16 points if No Trump has been bid. (This includes high cards and distribution.) The doubler should have strength in the three suits other than the one which has been bid, so that regardless of which suit his partner bids, he will have support for it.

Examine a few examples:

In each case you are South. East, your right-hand opponent, has opened with 1 Heart, and you hold:

(A) ♠ A Q 10 x   ♡ x   ◇ Q J 10 x   ♣ K J 9 x

(B) ♠ A J 9 x x ♡ x   ◇ K Q x x   ♣ A 10 x

(C) ♠ A Q x   ♡ x x   ◇ K J x   ♣ K Q J x x

(D) ♠ A x x   ♡ x x x   ◇ A K J x   ♣ x x x

(A) Double. Your hand is worth 15 points (13 in high cards and 2 for the singleton Heart). Your hand will make a reasonable dummy for any suit partner bids—Spades, Diamonds, or Clubs.

(B) Double. This is better than making a mere overcall of 1 Spade. Your hand is worth 16 points (14 in high cards and 2 for the singleton). It is a little too strong for a mere overcall.

(C) Double. Your hand is worth 17 points (16 in high cards and 1 for the doubleton). It is too good for a mere overcall of 2 Clubs.

(D) Pass. This hand is worth only 12 points.

Responding When Your Partner Makes a Take-out Double

As we stated before, the most important single consideration is that you *must not pass*.* As partner of the doubler, it is your duty to bid your best suit. But many times this suit will not be biddable. Suppose your partner has doubled an opening bid of 1 Spade, and you hold:

    ♠ x x   ♡ x x x   ◇ x x x   ♣ A 10 x x x

You are fortunate enough to have a biddable suit, and you bid 2 Clubs. But even if you had:

    ♠ x x x   ♡ x x x   ◇ x x x   ♣ 10 x x x

you would still bid 2 Clubs. If you pass, the opponents will play the hand at 1 Spade, doubled, and probably make their contract with a couple of overtricks. This would prove very expensive— surely more frightening than following orders and bidding your best suit, even when it is 10 x x x.

How do you determine which is your best suit? It is done on the basis of length. 10 9 x x x is better than K J x x. When you have two suits of the same length, usually four cards each, you may have to use your judgment. Suppose your partner doubles an opening bid of 1 Heart, and you have:

    ♠ J x x x   ♡ x x x   ◇ K 9 x x   ♣ x x

Your Diamonds are a little stronger than your Spades, but the better response to partner's double is 1 Spade. First, because in

---

* There is an exception. If you have a good bid yourself in the suit partner has doubled, you may pass, and the hand may be played at the doubled contract. For example:

Your partner has doubled 1 Spade, and you hold:

    ♠ Q J 10 9 8   ♡ x x   ◇ x x x   ♣ A x x

You may pass and play for penalties. You can win four tricks, and doubler should win three.

responding to take-out doubles we prefer to show a major suit. Second, with this weak hand we would prefer the cheapest possible bid (1 Spade). To show Diamonds you would have to bid at the two level.

Judging Your Hand When Partner Has Made a Take-out Double

Most players tend to undervalue their hand in this situation. My advice is always to adopt an optimistic attitude when your partner makes a take-out double.

If you have 6 points it is a fair hand.

If you have 9 points, it is a good hand.*

If you have 11 points, you have a probable game.

When you have 11 points and partner makes a take-out double, you should bid one more than is necessary.

For example:
You are South. West has opened with 1 Heart. North, your partner, has doubled. East has passed. You hold:

♠ K Q x x x   ♡ x x x   ◇ A J x   ♣ x x

Respond 2 Spades rather than one because your hand is worth 11 points (10 in high cards and 1 for the doubleton).

You are South. West has opened with 1 Heart. Your partner, North, has doubled. East has passed, and you hold:

* If you have a stopper in the suit bid by the opponents and about 9 points, you may respond with 1 No Trump.

(A)	♠ x x	♡ J x x x	◇ K J x x x	♣ x x
(B)	♠ Q x x x	♡ K Q x	◇ x x x	♣ x x x
(C)	♠ A J x x x	♡ x x x	◇ K Q x	♣ x x

Bid:

(A) 2 Diamonds. Your best suit.

(B) 1 Spade. Your best suit. This is better than responding with 1 No Trump.

(C) 2 Spades, one more Spade than is necessary. This denotes a strong hand. Your hand valued at Spades is worth 11 points (10 in high cards and 1 for the doubleton).

Subsequent Action by the Player Who Has Made the Take-out Double

Remember that your partner has been forced to bid and may have nothing. Don't let your blood pressure rise. It is preferable for you to incline toward pessimism rather than optimism. Be sure you have good trumps before you raise partner, for he may not have a biddable suit.

When you contemplate raising partner, bear this table in mind:

> With 16 points you may go to the 2 level
> With 19 points you may go to the 3 level
> With 22 points you may go to the 4 level

For example:
You are South. East has opened with 1 Heart; you have made a take-out double; West has passed; North, your partner, has

responded 1 Spade. East then passes. What action do you take?

(A)	♠ Q x x x	♡ x	◇ A J x x	♣ A Q x x
(B)	♠ K J x x	♡ x	◇ K Q J x	♣ A Q x x
(C)	♠ x x x x	♡ x x	◇ A Q x x	♣ A K x

(A) Raise to 2 Spades. Your hand is worth only 16 points* in support of Spades, and partner may have practically nothing, for he was forced to bid.

(B) You may raise to 3 Spades. Your hand is worth 19 points. If partner has some slight values he may go to four.

(C) Pass. Your hand is worth only 14 points, and you cannot have a game because partner couldn't have 12 points else he would have responded 2 Spades.

---

* Note that you now value your hand in support of a Spade bid, thus counting 3 points for the singleton Heart.

CHAPTER VIII

PENALTY DOUBLES

WHEN A DOUBLE is not intended for a take-out, it is known as a PENALTY DOUBLE. This is made in order to increase the penalty if the opposition does not succeed in fulfilling their contract. Doubling becomes especially important when the opponents are vulnerable. Then, if they are set two tricks not doubled, they lose only 200 points; but if you double and set them two tricks, the sting is 500 points.

How can you tell when your partner's double is intended for penalties rather than for a take-out?

If you have already made some kind of bid and your partner doubles, that is for penalties. For example: You open 1 Heart, and the next player bids 1 Spade. Your partner doubles. This double does not ask you to bid. That would be pointless, for you have already bid. The double announces that partner wishes to play against 1 Spade, which he thinks he can defeat. It is a penalty double.

If your partner doubles a contract such as 4 Hearts, that is for penalties.

The question will naturally arise: "How much do you need to make a penalty double?" That depends on a number of factors. The problem is attacked in a simple businesslike manner. "How many tricks have the opponents contracted for, and how many is our side reasonably expected to take?"

In doubling suit contracts one should not concentrate too much on point count but should consider, rather, only "sure" tricks.

If partner has not bid, you should count on him for nothing; and you must be able to win enough tricks in your own hand to defeat the contract.

If he has bid, you may count on him to win a certain number of tricks, depending upon the type of bid he has made. When partner has opened with one of a suit, you may count on him to win three tricks. When partner has opened with 1 No Trump, you may count on him to win four tricks. When partner has made a take-out double, count on him to win three tricks. When partner has given you a single raise, count on him to win one trick. When partner has made a mere overcall of the opponents' opening bid, count on him to win only one trick.

For example:

Your partner opens with 1 Heart, and your right-hand opponent overcalls with 1 Spade. You hold:

    ♠ K J 9 x   ♡ J x   ◇ A J 10 x   ♣ x x x

You should double. Since partner has already bid, this is for penalties. You expect to defeat the contract of 1 Spade, for you should win about three tricks in Spades and perhaps two in Diamonds. Since your partner as opener is expected to win three tricks, the opponents should be defeated by two. Incidentally, a reasonably good test as to whether your hand is worth a penalty double is this: After your partner opens, if the next hand makes a bid that you intended to make, you have a sound double.

Here is another example:

Partner opens with 1 Spade. Your right-hand opponent overcalls with 2 Diamonds. You hold:

    ♠ J x   ♡ A x x   ◇ Q 10 x x   ♣ K x x x

Against the Diamond contract you should win two tricks in trumps, one in Hearts, and probably one in Clubs. That is four tricks. Partner is expected to win three, yielding a total of seven, and therefore an expected penalty of two tricks. You should double. Some players make the mistake of bidding 2 No Trump in cases of this type in order to show that they have Diamonds well stopped. You will find that the penalty double, instead of the 2 No Trump bid, will prove highly profitable.

CHAPTER IX

SLAM BIDDING

THERE IS SOME question in my mind as to whether a separate heading is required for this subject. Bidding is an elaborate form of estimating or appraisal. When you bid 3 No Trump, you have estimated that your side has 26 points and that you will win nine tricks. When you bid 5 Diamonds, you have estimated that your side has 28 or 29 points and that you will win eleven tricks. Similarly, if you estimate that your partnership has about 34 points, you predict that you will win twelve tricks and therefore contract for a small slam.

However, certain safeguards may be necessary to determine whether or not the enemy can take two fast tricks against you when you contemplate a slam. Another and possibly more vital consideration is: "How good is our trump suit?" As a rule, it should be solid, but at the very most you must not expect to lose more than one trump trick.

If you have just a biddable suit and partner has raised it, it is not necessarily strong enough for slam purposes. Partner may have raised on x x x x or Q x x, and if your suit is not nearly solid, you may have to lose two tricks in trumps alone.

If you have supported partner with x x x x, do not act upon the belief that you have satisfactory trumps for a slam unless partner has rebid the suit *strongly*. If you have only three trumps for partner, they should be good ones, like A 10 x, K J x, or even Q J x, but be sure partner has rebid the suit before you suggest a slam in that suit. He might have only a four-card suit, and a seven-card trump holding is not recommended for slam purposes.

Then make sure you have sufficient material for slam purposes. The necessary material is 34 points in your current state of development. When you attain greater experience, you may try with 33 points.

Sometimes, when you realize that your partnership has the necessary 33 or 34 points and a satisfactory trump suit, you may fear to contract for slam lest the opponents have two Aces against you. In such cases you may employ the 4 NO TRUMP CONVENTION, popularly known as the Blackwood convention.

This convention (bid) provides that if one of the partners suddenly jumps to 4 No Trump when it is clear that a suit has been agreed upon as trumps, the 4 No Trump bid is artificial and asks partner how many Aces he has. Partner's responses are as follows:

With no Aces he bids	5 Clubs
With 1 Ace he bids	5 Diamonds
With 2 Aces he bids	5 Hearts
With 3 Aces he bids	5 Spades
With 4 Aces he bids	5 No Trump

Observe the following illustration:

♠ x
♡ K Q J 10 x
◊ K Q J
♣ Q 10 x x

NORTH

SOUTH

♠ K Q J x
♡ A 9 x
◊ x
♣ A K J x x

The bidding:

North	East	South	West
1 Heart	Pass	3 Clubs	Pass
3 Hearts	Pass	3 Spades	Pass
4 Clubs	Pass	4 No Trump	Pass
5 Clubs	Pass	5 Hearts	Pass
Pass	Pass		

North opens with 1 Heart. South's hand is worth about 20 points, and he therefore visualizes a slam, because even if partner has only 13 points, the partnership will have 33 points. The slam signal is given by jumping in a new suit, 3 Clubs. (See page 58.) North could raise his partner to 4 Clubs but prefers not to do anything aggressive and rebids his Hearts to show a rebiddable suit. South then shows his four-card suit, having bid the five-card suit first. North then returns to his partner's first-named suit, calling

4 Clubs. This presumably fixes Clubs as trumps, and when partner bids 4 No Trump he is saying, "Partner, please tell me how many Aces you have." North, having none, bids 5 Clubs. South therefore realizes that the opponents hold the Ace of Spades and the Ace of Diamonds. He can pass 5 Clubs if he chooses but prefers to return to the higher-ranking declaration of 5 Hearts.

In each of the following cases you have opened with 1 Spade. Partner has responded 2 No Trump. Indicate whether or not you may reasonably contemplate a slam.

(A) ♠ A K x x x   ♡ K Q x   ◇ J x   ♣ K x x
(B) ♠ A K J x   ♡ K J x x   ◇ A Q x   ♣ J x
(C) ♠ A K J x x   ♡ A J x   ◇ K Q x   ♣ Q 10

In each of the following cases you have opened with 1 Spade. Partner has responded 3 Spades. Indicate whether or not you may reasonably contemplate a slam.

(D) ♠ A K Q x   ♡ K J 10 x   ◇ A J x   ♣ x x
(E) ♠ A K J x   ♡ J 10 x x   ◇ K Q x x   ♣ x
(F) ♠ K Q J x x   ♡ A K x   ◇ x   ♣ A J x x

In each of the following cases your partner has opened with 1 No Trump. Indicate whether or not you may reasonably contemplate a slam.

(G) ♠ A x x   ♡ K x x   ◇ K Q x x   ♣ Q x x
(H) ♠ A Q x   ♡ Q x x   ◇ A Q x x   ♣ K J x
(I) ♠ K Q 10 x x   ♡ A J 10 x x   ◇ K x   ♣ x

(A) NO. Your hand is worth 16 points in high cards. Partner's response of 2 No Trump designates 13, 14, or 15. You will therefore have at the very most 31 points, and delusions of grandeur should not be entertained.

(B) YES. Your hand is worth 19 points in high cards. There may be a good chance for slam if partner has more than just the minimum of 13 points. If he has 15, the partnership will have 34 points.

(C) DEFINITELY YES. Your hand is worth 20 points in high cards. Even if partner has only 13 points (he may have 14 or 15), your partnership will have 33 points, and with a good five-card suit 33 points should serve as well as 34 without a five-card suit. You should, therefore, bid 6 No Trump directly.

(D) YES. Your hand is worth 19 points valued at a suit. Even if partner has only 13, you will be on the threshold of a slam; and if he has 15 or 16, it will be a virtual cinch, because the partnership will then have 34 or 35 points.

(E) NO. Your hand is worth 16 points (14 in high cards and 2 for the singleton). Even if partner's jump raise is maximum (16 points), you will have no more than 32.

(F) TO BE SURE! Your hand is worth 21 points.* Even if partner has only 13, you will have enough. You are strong enough to contract for slam yourself.

---

* At this stage it may be appropriate to refer to a principle which we have not previously discussed. When your partner has raised your suit, you should revalue your hand in the following manner: If your trump suit is 5 cards long, add 1 point for the fifth trump. If your suit is longer, add 2 additional points for the sixth card and 2 more points for the seventh card.

(G) NO. Partner's maximum is 18, so the partnership cannot have more than 32.

(H) YES. You have enough to bid a slam yourself. Even opposite a minimum 16-Point No Trump, you will have 34 points.

(I) YES. Valued for suit purposes, your hand is worth 16 points, which brings you into the slam zone.

CHAPTER X

GETTING TO GAME

WE ARE NOW presumably acquainted with the technique of opening the bidding and also with the rules for responding. By this time we have just gotten the bidding under way, and numerous problems may set in as the auction develops.

The primary object of the bidding will be expressed by the constant question, "Can my partner and I make game on this hand?" Remember that a contract of 3 No Trump will yield a trick score of 100 points below the line, which constitutes game. And it is very pleasant and profitable to make game in one hand wherever possible. Similarly, a bid of 4 Hearts or Spades will yield a trick score of 120, which constitutes game; and a bid of 5 Diamonds or 5 Clubs produces game (100 trick score).

If the bidding is conducted properly, you will be able to estimate whether 4 Hearts or 5 Clubs or 3 No Trump can be made on a particular hand. It is largely a matter of addition. By adding your holdings to those which partner has shown, you will have a fairly good idea of the combined assets.

If you and your partner can produce combined assets of 26 points, you should reach game, provided you are satisfied with partner's suit, or he is satisfied with yours, or you both are satisfied with No Trump.

Let us examine some illustrations:

Your partner opens the bidding with 1 Heart. You have no special support for Hearts, but you have about 8 points in high cards in the other suits. You say to yourself, "I know partner's hand is worth at least 13 points, and so far I can visualize only 21 points. So there seems no purpose to be accomplished by my bidding." However, that is not so, for partner need not have just 13. He might easily have 18 points, in which case your partnership would have the necessary 26 points, permitting you to make 3 No Trump. It is your duty, therefore, to tell partner that you have some moderate strength (6 to 9 points) by bidding 1 No Trump. Partner will count his hand, and he may realize that there is no chance for game, in which case he will discontinue the bidding. If he thinks there is a chance for game, he will keep on bidding. If he is sure there is game, he will bid it.

Example:

Opener	*Responder*
♠ x x	♠ Q J x
♡ A Q x	♡ K x x
◊ A K J x x	◊ 10 x x x
♣ A Q x	♣ J 10 x

Opener bids 1 Diamond. Responder, having 7 points, keeps the bidding open by bidding 1 No Trump. Opener now says to himself, "My partner has at least 6 points (6 to 9). I have 20. We therefore have 26 points, and since I am satisfied with No Trump, I shall bid for game (3 No Trump)."

On the other hand, this might have been the case:

Opener	*Responder*
♠ x x	♠ Q J x
♡ J x x	♡ K x x
◊ A K J x x	◊ 10 x x x
♣ A Q x	♣ J 10 x

Opener bids 1 Diamond. Responder bids 1 No Trump. Opener now says to himself, "My partner has at most 9 points. Since I have only 15 points in high cards, we cannot possibly have 26 points, because 24 is the most that can be accounted for. There is no possible game, and therefore I will quit at the cheapest place, which is 1 No Trump. There is no need for me to bid 2 Diamonds."

When responder cannot be *sure* at the start that there is game but has some hope that there *may* be game in the hand, he should arrange to bid in such a manner that he will get another chance. How can he do this? By making a bid which is a ONE-ROUND FORCE—that is, one which opener is not permitted to pass. When responder names a new suit, opener must bid once more; so responder is assured of another chance by bidding a new suit.

When the bidding reverts to the opener, he may be in such a position that he wishes to make sure that responder bids at least once more. How does he do it?

Opener	Responder
♠ A x	♠ K Q x x
♡ A K Q x x	♡ x x
♢ A K J x	♢ x x x
♣ x x	♣ Q J 10 x

Opener bids 1 Heart, and his partner responds 1 Spade. Opener has such a strong hand that he wishes to reach game even if responder has only 6 points. But opener is not sure what the best final contract will be. He wishes to hear further from partner. Opener's second suit is Diamonds, but if his rebid is 2 Diamonds, responder might not go on even though it is a new suit. Remember that when responder bids a new suit, opener *must* bid again; but when opener bids a new suit, responder need not bid again if he does not choose to. If opener wishes to force responder to bid

again he must *jump in a new suit*. In this case, opener would bid
3 Diamonds (a jump shift). This forces partner to bid again and
to keep bidding till game is reached.

The bidding so far has been:

Opener	*Responder*
1 Heart	1 Spade
3 Diamonds	

Responder, if he likes Hearts better, may return to 3 Hearts.
If responder does not like either Hearts or Diamonds, he may
wish to rebid his Spades. This will show a good suit of at least
five cards. If responder does not have strong Spades and does not
like either Hearts or Diamonds, he will bid 3 No Trump, which
actually took place in the hand shown above.

CHAPTER XI

PLAY OF THE HAND

IF YOUR SIDE has made the highest bid and you are the one who first named the suit, you will become declarer and must play the hand. Uppermost in your mind must be your objective. "How many tricks must I win?" is the prime question. If your contract is 4 Spades, your goal is ten tricks. If the final bid was 3 Hearts, your objective is nine tricks.

In playing a hand one never loses sight of the rank of the cards. Remember that if you have the King, Queen and Jack of a suit, you cannot be sure of winning tricks in that suit before you have permitted the enemy to win a trick with their Ace. When the King is given up to the adverse Ace, your Queen and Jack will be promoted to winning rank and will take two tricks.

When the dummy is spread, before playing impulsively to the trick, map your program for winning the required number of tricks. In a contract of 4 Hearts, for example, you may see that you have eight tricks which you can take immediately. You must therefore look around for some method of building up two more, and it may take time. Before constructing these two tricks you may have to give some to the opponents. Suppose, for example, you are South playing this hand at a contract of 4 Spades.

```
              ♠ 10 7 5
              ♡ A 8 3
              ◇ A 8 4 2
              ♣ 9 8 5

  ♠ 6 4 3 2        N         ♠ 9
  ♡ Q J 10                   ♡ 9 7 6 5 4
  ◇ K Q 7    W         E     ◇ J 10 6 5
  ♣ K 4 3          S         ♣ A 7 2

              ♠ A K Q J 8
              ♡ K 2
              ◇ 9 3
              ♣ Q J 10 6
```

The opening lead is the Queen of Hearts which you win in your own hand with the King. You can see that you can win five tricks by leading Spades, two tricks by winning with the King and Ace of Hearts, and one trick with the Ace of Diamonds. That amounts to eight. You will need two more and with patience you can win them if you permit the adversaries first to win a trick with the King and another one with the Ace. The Queen of Clubs will presumably force out the King, the Jack will then force out the Ace, and your 10 and 9 will become ranking cards and win two tricks. Observe that after drawing all the enemy trumps you must not take in your Ace of Diamonds and your Ace of Hearts first, before working on the Clubs. As soon as you have drawn the trumps, you must play a Club first, since when the opponents play back a Diamond or a Heart, you win the trick with the Ace and play another Club. As an interesting experiment, take a deck of cards and place the complete deal on the table and play all four hands yourself. In doing so, play all your own high cards first before you play any Clubs and notice what a difference there will be in the number of tricks you will win (provided East and West do not play their Ace and King of Clubs until they are forced to do so).

Declarer can win tricks in several ways. We have just shown how he wins two tricks by driving out two high cards in the possession of the opponents and builds up high cards of his own. Declarer can also win tricks with very low cards, which can be built up by exhausting the opposition of that suit. For example, you are South playing at a Spade contract, and you have drawn all the trumps. Your dummy contains the following holding in Clubs: A 8 7 6 5. You have in your own hand 4 3 2 in Clubs. In fact, that suit is distributed around the table as follows:

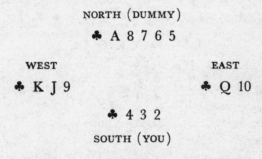

NORTH (DUMMY)

♣ A 8 7 6 5

WEST   EAST

♣ K J 9   ♣ Q 10

♣ 4 3 2

SOUTH (YOU)

You play the 2 of Clubs. West plays the 9, and you play the 5 from dummy. East wins the trick with the 10 and leads back some other suit which you win. You then play the 3 of Clubs. West plays the Jack, and you play the 6 from dummy. East wins with the Queen. East leads some other suit and you win. Now when you play your last Club, the 4, West must play the King (the only Club outstanding). You win with the Ace, and now no one has any Clubs left, so the 8 and 7 are ranking cards, and you win two tricks with them.

Declarer can also win tricks with little cards by trumping small cards in the dummy. For example, you are South, declarer at a contract of 4 Spades.

NORTH (DUMMY)

♠ 10 6 3
♡ 7
♢ A 7 5 3 2
♣ 8 7 5 2

WEST

♠ 9 7 4
♡ Q J 10 6
♢ 8 4
♣ A Q 10 4

EAST

♠ 8 5
♡ K 9 5 3 2
♢ Q J 10 9
♣ K J

♠ A K Q J 2
♡ A 8 4
♢ K 6
♣ 9 6 3

SOUTH (YOU)

West leads the Queen of Hearts and you win with the Ace. If you draw all the trumps, you will win five Spade tricks, the Ace and King of Diamonds and the Ace of Hearts, a total of eight tricks and two short of your contract. In other words, you will lose three Club tricks and you will also lose the two little Hearts. Now you cannot prevent the loss of the three little Clubs, but you can do something about the two little Hearts. Notice that after you have played the Ace of Hearts, the dummy has no more of that suit, so you may trump the small Hearts with dummy's little trumps. After winning with the Ace, you play the 4 of Hearts from your hand and the 3 of Spades from dummy, winning the trick by ruffing (trumping).

You then wish to return to your hand, so you play the 2 of Diamonds from dummy and the King of Diamonds from your own hand. You then play the 8 of Hearts from your hand and a Spade from dummy, winning the trick by ruffing. Now you play the Ace, King and Queen of trumps so that the opposition, East and West, have no more. You will therefore have scored ten tricks, five Spades in your own hand, the Ace and King of Diamonds, the Ace of Hearts, and two more tricks when you trumped the two little Hearts in dummy. To put it in another way, you lost only three of the thirteen tricks, namely the three small Clubs in your own hand.

For the last few pages, we have been discussing basic tactics when you are declarer. Let us now take a few moments to examine questions of play when an opponent has become declarer, and you are the defender.

Your objectives are somewhat similar. If the adversaries have taken the contract by bidding 4 Spades, their goal is ten tricks, but your goal is four tricks because it will take four tricks to defeat them. You must set your sights, therefore, to win not merely one or two or three tricks, but at least four. And if, incidentally, you can win more than four, that is so much the better. But your objective is four.

Suppose the opponents have bid 5 Clubs and you have

♠ K Q 6
♡ A 9 5 3
◊ A 4 3 2
♣ 8 7

Your objective is three tricks, for the adversaries need eleven. You can count on winning one trick with the Ace of Hearts and one with the Ace of Diamonds. You will then need one more trick, and you hope eventually to take a trick in Spades. Of course you cannot win a Spade trick immediately because the enemy has the Ace of Spades. But your King will force out the Ace. And then your Queen will be the highest Spade remaining and will be of winning rank.

It would be poor tactics to play your two Aces first and then hope to take a Spade trick later. You should first play the King of Spades. In order to win this trick, declarer will have to use his Ace. Now when he plays some other suit you will obtain the lead and win tricks with the Queen of Spades and your two Aces.

Here is the complete hand:

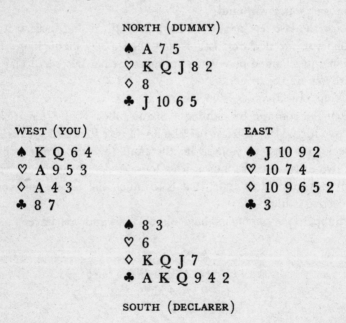

NORTH (DUMMY)

♠ A 7 5
♡ K Q J 8 2
♦ 8
♣ J 10 6 5

WEST (YOU)

♠ K Q 6 4
♡ A 9 5 3
♦ A 4 3
♣ 8 7

EAST

♠ J 10 9 2
♡ 10 7 4
♦ 10 9 6 5 2
♣ 3

♠ 8 3
♡ 6
♦ K Q J 7
♣ A K Q 9 4 2

SOUTH (DECLARER)

It may be interesting to take a deck of cards and spread them on the table according to the above diagram. You are West. Now, try playing one of your Aces first and then play the hand as though you were declarer—playing with all the cards exposed. You will see that declarer, South, will succeed in winning eleven tricks. Or, to put it in another way, he will lose only two tricks, one in Hearts and one in Diamonds, for he will lose no Spade trick.

Let us assume you have played the Ace of Hearts, which wins. When you see the dummy, you then decide to play the King of Spades. This is taken by the Ace in dummy. Declarer then plays the Ace and King of Clubs, and now neither you nor your partner has any Clubs (trumps). Declarer may then play a Club to dummy's Jack. Now the lead is in the dummy and declarer plays the King of Hearts, and since he has no Hearts in his own hand, he may discard the 8 of Spades (he has already played the 3 when West at the second trick led the King of Spades and North played the Ace). He then plays the Queen of Hearts from dummy and discards the 7 of Diamonds from his own hand.

Now declarer has no Hearts, no Spades, three good trumps and the King, Queen, Jack of Diamonds. He must lose one trick to the Ace of Diamonds and he makes his contract.

The Opening Lead

In every hand of contract bridge there are thirteen leads, one to each trick. The lead to the first trick is called the OPENING LEAD. Whenever your right-hand opponent becomes the declarer, it will be your duty to make that opening lead before the dummy is spread. Leading is not always a privilege, it may sometimes prove to be a burden. For it is frequently a disadvantage to be forced to lead from certain combinations of cards. On the other hand, there are some holdings from which it is a pleasure to lead. Suppose, for example, you hold Ace, King, Queen, and another of the same suit. If you lead the King, you are quite sure that you will win the trick; and, when the dummy is spread, showing you one of the opponents' hands, you may gain a better idea of what to lead at the second trick. Similarly, if you hold the King, Queen, Jack, 10, and another card of the same suit, you have a very attractive lead, for the King will force out the Ace, and you will then hold the commanding cards in that suit. In other words, the most desirable leads are those from a sequence of cards. On the other hand, when you lead from a suit containing high cards which are not in sequence, you may be at a disadvantage.

For example:

You are seated in the West position; and since South has made the highest bid, he is the declarer. You must, therefore, make the opening lead. Let us suppose you choose to lead a little Diamond.

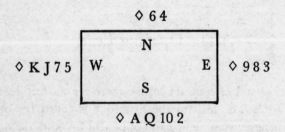

You will observe that South will be able to win the first trick with the 10. If you had led some other suit and waited for North and

South to lead Diamonds, they would have made only the Ace, and you would have taken all the other tricks in Diamonds.

Similarly,

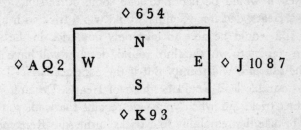

$\diamond$ 6 5 4

$\diamond$ A Q 2   W   N   E $\diamond$ J 10 8 7

S

$\diamond$ K 9 3

If, as West, you lead the Ace of Diamonds, South will win a trick with his King. But if you lead some other suit and wait for your partner, East, to lead the Jack of Diamonds, declarer will lose his King and will take no tricks in the suit.

Difference Between Suit Leads and No Trump Leads

In selecting your opening lead, you will be influenced by whether your adversary is playing at a suit contract or at No Trump. Let us assume that you are West in the following diagram and must make the opening lead.

$\heartsuit$ J 6 3

$\heartsuit$ A Q 10 5 2   W   N   E $\heartsuit$ 9 8 7

S

$\heartsuit$ K 4

Whether or not you should lead a Heart or select some other suit for your lead would depend upon whether the contract were No Trump or a suit. If you were leading against a contract of 4 Spades, it would be better to lead some other suit, for if you lead a Heart, declarer (South) would win a trick with his King, and you would be able to take only one trick in the suit, for when you try to win the third round, declarer will have no more of the suit and will trump. But if the contract is No Trump, a very desirable lead would be the 5 of Hearts. Declarer will win the first trick, but when your side regains the lead, you will be able to take the remaining four tricks in the suit. Remember that South cannot take these tricks from you by trumping, for at a No Trump contract there are no trumps.

To summarize: Against suit contracts you must be wary of leading from those suits in which you have high cards which are not in sequence; for by the time your high cards become good, declarer will have no more, and will trump. But in No Trump contracts you need not entertain the same fear. Eventually your high cards will become winners.

If you hold A K 7 4 2 against a suit contract, you can hope to cash only the Ace and King, and you must do so early. If you lead a little one first, declarer may win with the Queen, and then, when you try to cash your high cards, he may trump. But at No Trump you may lead the 4 because the Ace and King will be good any time at all, and perhaps the 7 and 2 as well. Remember the importance of little cards of a long suit when the contract is No Trump. The best way to do battle against No Trump is to establish a long suit.

It is therefore wise to lead your longest suit against No Trump, so that, when no one else has any more of that suit, your little cards will win tricks.

When Partner Has Bid a Suit

While there are certain combinations of cards from which you would not normally lead (such as A Q 4), if your partner has bid that suit, you should lead it unhesitatingly. Now you do not fear that declarer has the King, but are reasonably safe in assuming that partner has the King.

Generally speaking, therefore, your best opening (with very few exceptions) is your partner's suit, even though you haven't very much in his suit and have some suit of your own. When you have a very strong suit, you may choose to lead it rather than the one partner has bid.

The Card to Lead

When you have chosen the suit to lead, you must then pick the proper card of that suit to lead. The choice of the proper card to lead will sometimes depend upon whether you are leading against No Trump or against a suit. Many of these leads depend upon accepted conventions.

For example, suppose that you hold a suit containing both the Ace and King. It is your intention to lead one of the high ones. The Ace and King, when in one hand, are, of course, of equal value. Which is the proper card to lead? The answer is the King because of the information it will convey to partner. When you win the trick with the King, partner will surmise that you have the Ace. But if you lead the Ace, partner will have no idea who has the King.

When you choose to lead a suit which is headed by a complete sequence of honors (at least three touching honors other than the Ace), it is conventionally correct to lead the card which is the top of the sequence. The underlined card is led from each of the following:

K Q J x   Q J 10 x   J 10 9 x

As we have pointed out before, it is better, when playing against a suit bid, to avoid leading a suit which is headed by the Ace but missing the King. (When your partner has bid that suit, the objection disappears.) But if you find that you must lead the suit, lead the Ace and not a little one. For if you lead a small card, you may never win a trick with your Ace. It may be trumped by declarer at a later time.

But if the contract is No Trump, leading a low card away from an Ace is not dangerous; for whenever you subsequently obtain the lead, you will be able to cash the Ace, which cannot be trumped. When you lead from a long suit at No Trump, you select the fourth highest card, unless the suit happens to be headed by a sequence, or by three of the honors. To illustrate, the underlined card is the accepted conventional lead against No Trump from each of the following:

K 8 7 5 3   A 9 5 3 2   A Q 7 4 2   K Q 10 6 3

Q J 10 6 4   K Q J 8 2   K J 9 8 3   A J 8 7 3

The Card to Lead of Partner's Suit

The practice of leading the fourth highest card also applies when you are leading the suit which partner has bid. When you have the Ace of partner's suit and several other cards, you should lead the Ace if it is a suit contract. But if the contract is No Trump, you lead the fourth highest. This helps partner to determine how the suit is distributed, for you will be telling him how many you have.

If you have three cards of partner's suit, headed by a single honor, it is customary to lead the lowest. However, from a two-card holding, the higher is always led, and if you have three small ones, lead the highest. When you have two honors in sequence in partner's suit, you lead the higher, except in the case of the Ace-King.

In the following table, the underlined card is the one of partner's bid suit which should be led against No Trump:

A 2̲	6̲ 5 4	A 6 3̲ 2	5 4 3̲ 2
K 2̲	A 6 2̲	K 6 3̲ 2	9 6 4 3̲ 2
Q 2̲	K 6̲ 2	Q 6 3̲ 2	Q J 6̲ 2
9̲ 2	Q 6̲ 2	J 6 3̲ 2	K Q 6̲ 2
9̲ 6 2	J 6̲ 2	9 6 3̲ 2	J̲ 10 6 2

Opening Lead Table*

(Leads of Suits Not Bid by Partner)

Holding in Suit	Against No Trump	Against Trump Bids
A K Q J	A	K
A K Q x x x	A	K
A K Q x x	K	K
A K Q x	K	K
A K x	K	K
A K J 10 x	J	K
A K J 10	A	K
A K J x	A	K
A K 10 x	K	K
A K J x x	x	K
A K J x x x x	A	K
A K x x x x	x	K
A K 10 9	10	K
A K 10 9 x x	10	K
A K x x x	x	K
A Q J x x	Q	A
K Q J x x	K	K
K Q 10 x x	K	K
K Q 7 4 2	4	K
Q J 10 x x	Q	Q
Q J 9 x x	Q	Q
Q J 7 4 2	4	4
J 10 9 x x	J	J
J 10 8 x x	J	J
J 10 7 4 2	4	4

* The following are the accepted, conventional leads from these holdings. It is suggested that you do not concern yourself too much, at the present stage of your development, with the reasons underlying them. Learn them by rote, if necessary; or refer to them, if in doubt.

Holding in Suit	Against No Trump	Against Trump Bids
10 9 8	10	10
10 9 7 4	4	10
A Q 10 9 x	10	A
A Q 8 7 4 2	7	A
A J 10 8 2	J	A
A 10 9 8 2	10	A
K J 10 7 2	J	J
K 10 9 7 2	10	10
Q 10 9 7 2	10	10
A J 4	4	4
K J 4	4	4
K 7 4	4	4
Q 10 4	4	4
J 7 4	4	4
K 9 8 7	7	7

The Rule of Eleven

The Rule of Eleven is an easy and rapid method of calculation, to be employed when it is known that the opening leader has chosen the fourth best card of the suit he has led.

When the size of the card is subtracted from eleven, the remainder is equal to the number of cards in that suit (outside the leader's hand) which can beat the card led. For example, if a 6 is led, there are five cards of the suit higher than the 6 which are not in the leader's hand. Thus:

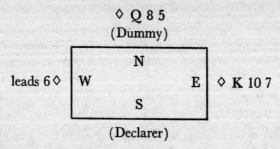

♢ Q 8 5
(Dummy)

leads 6 ♢

♢ K 10 7

(Declarer)

West leads the 6 of Diamonds, and dummy plays the 8. East
subtracts six from eleven, which leaves five; that means that
North and East and South together have only five cards which
can beat the 6. East has three himself, and dummy has two, so
South cannot have a card to beat the 6, and East knows that he
can win the trick with the 10 and need not, therefore, waste the
King.

Another illustration:

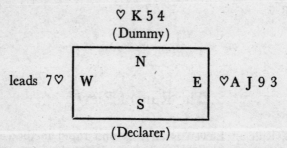

♡ K 5 4
(Dummy)

leads 7 ♡

♡ A J 9 3

(Declarer)

West leads the 7 of Hearts, and North plays the 4. East plays the
3, knowing partner's 7 will win the trick. 11—7=4. There are
four cards outside of leader's hand which can beat the 7. East
has three and dummy has one. South, therefore, has none. The
only cards higher than the 7 that are unaccounted for are the 8,
10, and Q. West must have all of them if the 7 is his fourth
highest card.

The Play of the Hand by Declarer

It may seem like placing too great a burden on the beginner to ask him to map out a campaign when he embarks on the play of any hand. Nevertheless, it can do no harm to develop good habits early, even though they may not be successful at first. When the bidding is completed, the opening lead has been made, and the dummy spread face up on the table, the wise declarer takes stock of his resources and maps out his plan of action. Since your sole object, as declarer, is to secure enough tricks to fulfill contract, you should:

(A) When playing a hand at a suit contract, try to estimate your probable and possible *losers*. If these total more than you can afford to lose and still fulfill contract, try to devise a plan to eliminate these losers.

(B) When playing a No Trump contract, count your sure and probable *winners*. If these are less than you require to fulfill contract, cast about to see which suits may possibly produce an extra winner. Always bear in mind that these winners must be obtained before the defenders are able to capture enough tricks to defeat you. This is what is known as TIMING.

Another good habit to develop is not to play a card from dummy after the opening lead until some sound plan has been formulated. A player who relies on instinct alone must fall into a great many errors at the Bridge table. A player must constantly ask himself the reason for making this play or that. "Why am I doing this?" is the basis of all correct play.

Leading Toward High Cards

It is an elementary principle of play that best results will be obtained by leading toward high-card combinations. For example:

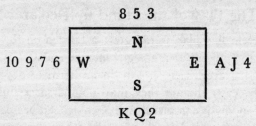

Here you are trying to win tricks with both the King and Queen. That can be done only if East holds the Ace, and provided he is compelled to play before you. The proper procedure is to lead a small card from the North hand. If East plays the Ace, your troubles are over. If he plays small, you win with the Queen and enter the North hand again, with a high card in some other suit, to repeat the process. Note that if you had led the King out of your hand, you could have taken only one trick, with the Queen.

Leads Toward Tenaces

A TENACE is a combination of cards with the middle card, of what would otherwise be three touching cards, missing: A Q, K J, A Q 10, A J 10, K Q 10, etc. All suits containing a tenace should, if possible, be led up to rather than from. In other words, the lead should come from the weak holding up to the strong one.

K J 5

```
+---------------+
|       N       |
|               |
|       S       |
+---------------+
```

6 4 2

In this example, if you lead twice toward the K J 5, you win two tricks if West has both the Ace and Queen. You win one trick if West has either the Ace or Queen. But if you lead from the North hand toward the three small cards in the South hand, you will probably not win any tricks.

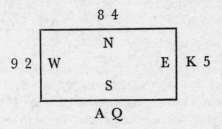

8 4

9 2   W   N   E   K 5

S

A Q

If South should improperly lead the Ace, East will follow suit with the 5, and East's King will subsequently win a trick. But if South, instead of leading from his own hand, gets over to dummy with some other suit and then leads from the North hand, East's King will be caught in a trap. If he plays the 5, South can win the trick by playing the Queen (the finesse). If he plays the King, South will, of course, win with the Ace and then the Queen.

Let us linger a moment over the term "finesse," a word which you will hear constantly during your Bridge-playing days. The definition of a finesse, in general terms, is the attempt to win a trick with a card when there is a higher card out against it. Observe the following examples:

	(1)			(2)	
	NORTH			NORTH	
	A K J			A Q J	
WEST		EAST	WEST		EAST
Q 6 3		10 8 4 2	K 6 3		10 8 4 2
	9 7 5			9 7 5	
	SOUTH			SOUTH	

(3)

NORTH

K J 10

WEST   EAST

Q 6 3   **A 8 4 2**

9 7 5

SOUTH

In each of these three diagrams, you are South and the lead at the moment is from your own hand: In case (1):

> You wish to win all three tricks. Two of them, the Ace and King, are sure tricks, but whether or not you can win with the Jack is problematical. If you play the Ace and King, each opponent will probably play small cards, and one of them will retain the Queen which will beat your Jack. After pondering the problem, you say to yourself, "If West has the Queen, I can win a trick with the Jack. I will lead the 5 from my hand and wait for West to play. If West plays a little card, I shall play the Jack and it will hold the trick." When you have done this, you have made a "finesse." That is, you have won a trick with the Jack when there was a higher card (the Queen) outstanding. You have finessed the Jack, or, to put it another way, you have finessed against the Queen which you had surrounded.

In case (2):

> You need all three tricks. If you play the Ace, you cannot expect the King to fall. So you say to yourself, "If West has the King, I can win all three tricks." So you lead the 5. West plays the 3. Dummy plays the Jack and holds the trick. You have successfully finessed the Jack. But your work is not done. If you now play the Ace, the King will not fall. You know that West has the King, so you must arrange to

get the play into South (your hand) to lead the suit again. You, therefore, play some other suit in which you have a commanding card in your own hand. When you get there, you lead the 7. West plays the 6, and you play the Queen from dummy, and it holds the trick. You have repeated the finesse against the King.

In case (3):

In this case you must lose one trick to the Ace, but you need two tricks. Your only hope is that West has the Queen. So you lead the 5 from the South hand. West plays the 3, and and you play the 10 from dummy. If East plays the Ace, he will win and lead something else. You then lead something which permits you to win in your own hand, and now lead the 7. West plays the 6 and you play the Jack from dummy, winning the trick or driving out the Ace.

Entry Cards

Though a player may understand the advantage of leading toward certain high-card combinations, he may be unable to apply his knowledge. This occurs when he cannot reach the hand from which he wishes to lead because that hand does not contain a card with which he can take a trick. In that case, he cannot place the lead—that is, gain entry to that hand and thereby advantageously lead toward the strong hand. In formulating your plan for playing the hand, you must try to note whether there are sufficient entry cards in the combined hands to enable you to make the necessary number of leads toward each high-card combination. When one hand holds an Ace and the other hand a King in the same suit, there is obviously entry into both hands. There are combinations which contain hidden entries, and the careful declarer will make good use of them.

For example:

♡ K Q 10

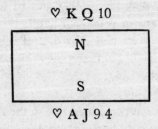

♡ A J 9 4

If you wish to lead a card, other than Hearts, three times from the North hand toward the South hand, you must be careful not to play the Ace of Hearts to an early trick, because that will destroy one of the entry cards in the North hand. You may enter dummy once by leading the 4 to the 10; another time by leading the 9 to the Queen; and a third time by leading the Jack to the King. Of course, you will subsequently return to the South hand with some other suit in order to cash the Ace. Observe that North has three entry cards, the King, the Queen and the 10.

Examine the following case:

♠ x x x
♡ x x x
◇ x x x
♣ A K Q 3

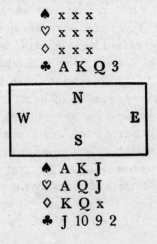

♠ A K J
♡ A Q J
◇ K Q x
♣ J 10 9 2

If a Spade is opened by West, note that it will be advantageous to lead twice toward South's Heart holding and twice toward South's Diamond holding. There are apparently only three cards of entry in the North hand, the Ace, the King and the Queen. However, there are only five Clubs outstanding in opponents' combined hands; and if these divide 3-2, which is normal, they can be picked up in three leads. Therefore, South's first play at the second trick should be the 9 of Clubs, and North should win with the Queen. The second lead of the Club suit should be the 10 of Clubs, which North wins with the King. If both opponents have followed to the two Club leads, there is only one more Club outstanding. Therefore, on the third lead of Clubs South can overtake the Jack of Clubs with North's Ace, which will be the third entry card. Now the 2 of Clubs can be led to North's 3 to provide the fourth entry card. This series of plays enables North to lead four times toward the South hand. On the other hand, if North's 3 of Clubs is played on either Jack, 10, or 9 in the South hand, North will be able to gain the lead only three times.

The Finesse

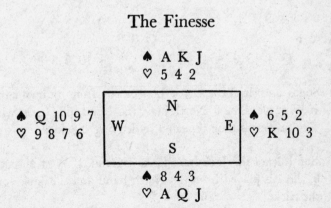

South is declarer and would like to win all six tricks. The lead is in his hand. He can succeed only if East has the King of Hearts and West the Queen of Spades. He therefore must enter dummy by playing a Spade to the Jack, which wins. He leads a Heart, and if East plays low, South wins with the Jack. This is known as a FINESSE (winning a trick with a card when there is a higher card out against it). Declarer is said to have finessed the Jack, or finessed against the King. He re-enters dummy with a Spade and this time finesses the Queen of Hearts, to win all the tricks.

When to Finesse

THE COMBINATION FINESSE

We have demonstrated the finesse when the Ace and Queen were in the same hand, or the Ace, King and Jack were in the same hand. It is also possible to finesse when the Ace and Queen are in different hands.

	(A)			(B)	
	A 9 7 4			A K 9 4	
K 8 6		5 2	Q 8 6		7 2
	Q J 10 3			J 10 5 3	

(A)   South must lead the Q (or Jack or 10) from his own hand. If West plays the 6, North plays the 4 and the Queen wins. The process is then repeated by leading the Jack.

(B)   South leads the Jack from his own hand. If West plays the 6, the 4 is played from the North hand and the Jack holds the trick.

But in the following example there is no finesse:

A 9 7 4

J 10 8   K 2

Q 6 5 3

South must not play the Queen. If he does so, he must lose at least two tricks. In the present case if he leads the Queen, West plays low, and East wins with the King. Declarer must still lose one more trick since the Jack and the 10 are outstanding. In playing this combination of cards, South should say to himself, "I wish the King to be with East." He, therefore, leads the 3 from his own hand and plays the Ace from dummy. North then plays the 4 and East wins with the King as West plays the 10. Now there is only one card out, the Jack, and that must fall under the Queen next time so that declarer loses only one trick and wins three.

"That's all very true," you may say, "but what if West had held the King?" Very well, I shall let you have your way. Here it is:

A 9 7 4

K 10 2   J 8

Q 6 5 3

You will have gained nothing by playing the Queen. If you do, West will play the King, dummy the Ace, and you will still have to lose to both the 10 and the Jack.

The object of finessing is to capture an adverse card which is missing from a tenace held by the declarer. In some cases the location of that card has become obvious either through the bidding or some previous incident in the play. In the absence of any such indication, the question of when a finesse should be tried and when it should be refused is not always easy to answer. But here is a table which may serve you as a guide:

Holding	Total Cards of Suit in Declarer's TWO Hands	Your Play
Ace-Queen	11	Ace
Ace-Queen	10 or less	Queen
Ace-King-Jack	9 or more	King
Ace-King-Jack	8 or less	Jack
Ace-Queen-10	9 or 10	Queen
Ace-Queen-10	8 or less	10

As an exercise in leading up to various card combinations, the following complete example may prove helpful. I suggest that you lay out the cards in these exercises and play them over.

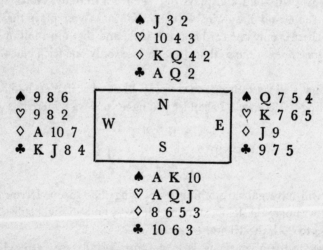

```
              ♠ J 3 2
              ♡ 10 4 3
              ◇ K Q 4 2
              ♣ A Q 2

♠ 9 8 6         N          ♠ Q 7 5 4
♡ 9 8 2     W       E      ♡ K 7 6 5
◇ A 10 7                   ◇ J 9
♣ K J 8 4       S          ♣ 9 7 5

              ♠ A K 10
              ♡ A Q J
              ◇ 8 6 5 3
              ♣ 10 6 3
```

South is playing a No Trump contract. West's opening lead is the 4 of Clubs. This minor suggestion is offered to you: Play low from dummy and you will win the trick with the 10. Diamonds must be led from the hand which is weak in Diamonds (South) toward the high cards. South leads the 5 of Diamonds, West plays the 7, and the dummy's Queen wins. Now,

Hearts must be led from the dummy hand toward the South hand, so the 3 is played, East plays the 5, and South plays the Jack, which wins. Now another Diamond, this time the 6, is led toward dummy. West plays the ten, and dummy wins with the King. Since the Ace is the only Diamond out, dummy plays the 2 and South the 8. Notice that South retains the 3 of Diamonds and North the 4, so if for any reason declarer wishes to enter dummy, he may do so with the little Diamond. West then plays the 8 of Clubs; dummy plays the Queen, which holds the trick. In an effort to avoid losing a trick to the Queen of Spades, declarer plays the 2 of Spades from dummy, and when East plays the 4, South plays the 10 and wins the trick. Now he leads the 3 of Diamonds over to the 4 in dummy and leads another Heart. East plays low, and when the Queen wins, declarer claims the rest of the tricks.

Ruffing

As a general principle, it is not profitable for declarer to use up his own trumps for the purpose of ruffing losing cards. The theory of the ruff is to make a trick with a trump which would otherwise be useless. When the dummy has small trumps and one or more of dummy's trumps can be used separately before trumps are drawn, they will be tricks in addition to the trump tricks in the declarer's hand. The following example will illustrate this point:

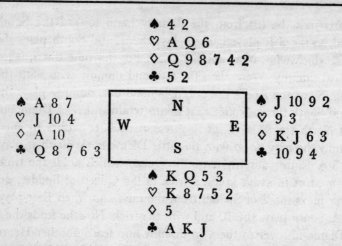

♠ 4 2
♡ A Q 6
◇ Q 9 8 7 4 2
♣ 5 2

♠ A 8 7   ♠ J 10 9 2
♡ J 10 4   ♡ 9 3
◇ A 10   ◇ K J 6 3
♣ Q 8 7 6 3   ♣ 10 9 4

♠ K Q 5 3
♡ K 8 7 5 2
◇ 5
♣ A K J

South is declarer and Hearts are trumps. West opens a Club. Notice that South can lead Spades, and after West takes his Ace, South can ruff a third round of Spades with dummy's 6. The 6 of Hearts has no value as a high card but can be used to ruff out or save this loser.

South could also ruff his last Spade, but it would not save a trick, for he would use dummy's Queen of Hearts to ruff it, and the Heart Queen is needed to draw the opponents' trumps.

Ducking

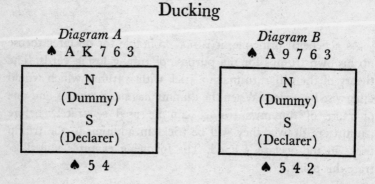

Diagram A
♠ A K 7 6 3

N
(Dummy)

S
(Declarer)

♠ 5 4

Diagram B
♠ A 9 7 6 3

N
(Dummy)

S
(Declarer)

♠ 5 4 2

In diagram A, assume that you are playing a No Trump contract and that the North hand has no other entry cards aside from the Spades. You are anxious to take four tricks in dummy's suit. How is this to be done? Since your opponents have six Spades, your only hope is that each of them will have three. If you play the Ace, King, and another, the two remaining Spades will be good, but you will have no means of getting over to dummy to use them. The proper procedure, therefore, is to give the opponents their trick at the beginning, rather than at the end. Play a small card, allowing the opponents to win the first trick by playing a low Spade from dummy. If the suit then does divide 3-3, the Ace and King left in dummy will clear the suit, and you will be enabled to take four Spade tricks.

In diagram B, assume that you need three tricks in the suit shown, with no other entry cards in the North hand. Since the opponents have five cards between them to the King-Queen-Jack-10, you will necessarily have to lose two tricks in the suit. Permit the opponents to win the first two tricks in the suit, conserving your Ace. If the suit does divide 3-2, the Ace, if played on the third trick, will pick up the one remaining card in the suit, and you will be enabled to win three tricks in the suit.

Another play which becomes important when dummy is lacking in entries is illustrated in the following example:

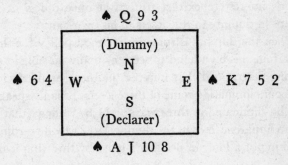

♠ Q 9 3

(Dummy)

N

♠ 6 4   W   E   ♠ K 7 5 2

S

(Declarer)

♠ A J 10 8

The lead is in dummy, which has no other entries. South wishes to win all the tricks by finessing against East's King; but if he is forced to win one of the early tricks in his own hand, he will not be able to repeat the finesse. He must, therefore, strive to retain the lead in dummy as long as possible. This can be done in two ways. If North leads the Queen, and East fails to cover with the King, South must play the 10 or Jack under it. North will hold the trick and is then in position to play the 9, and South may now underplay with the 8. In this way, the lead has been retained in dummy till the end. Another way is to lead the 9 from dummy and play the 8 from South. Dummy then follows with the Queen, and if East does not cover, the lead remains in dummy. If East covers with the King, the problem is over.

Management of Hands on Offense

Let us examine the following illustrations to demonstrate the development of a hand both at suit play and at No Trump.

In our first example we shall consider declarer's play at a contract of 4 Hearts.

In playing suit contracts it is very important to decide early in the hand whether or not the opponents' trumps should be extracted from them. Whether or not this is proper procedure depends on a number of factors. Generally speaking, it is to declarer's interest to extract trumps at once unless he needs the trumps in dummy to ruff losers in his own hand.

When the dummy is spread, it is good policy for the declarer to examine his own hand to see how many possible losers he has. Having determined that number, he then should decide how to go about eliminating some of these losers. Broadly speaking, losers may be eliminated in three ways: (1) by ruffing (that is, trumping an apparent loser in the dummy); (2) by discarding (that is, disposing of a loser in declarer's hand by throwing it upon some

card in dummy which has become established); (3) by finessing.
Example:

> Dummy
> ♠ J 10 7 2
> ♡ Q 7 4
> ◇ 7
> ♣ A J 9 6 5
>
> Declarer
> ♠ A 6
> ♡ A J 10 9 8 6
> ◇ A 3 2
> ♣ 3 2

In the above illustration South is declarer at a contract of 4
Hearts. West's opening lead has been the King of Diamonds.
Now, let us examine the possible losers in declarer's hand. In
Spades there is one loser, the 6 of Spades. In Hearts we must
count one loser, because of the possibility that the King of Hearts
will win a trick. In Diamonds declarer has two losers; the Ace
will win, but the 3 and the Deuce are potential losers. In Clubs
there is one loser, for while dummy's Ace will take care of the
Deuce of Clubs, the 3 of Clubs is a loser. Inasmuch as there are
five possible losers, declarer, if he is to succeed in making his contract of 4 Hearts, must reduce these losers to three.

Now, which losers can he eliminate? In Spades he will have
to lose one trick; in Clubs there is no way to avoid losing a trick;
but the two losers in Diamonds can be avoided by ruffing them
in dummy. Therefore, declarer wins the King of Diamonds with
the Ace and immediately plays the Deuce of Diamonds and ruffs
in dummy with the 7 of trumps. He then returns to his hand with
the Ace of Spades and leads the 3 of Diamonds, ruffing it in
dummy with the Queen of trumps.

Since two of the five original losers have now been eliminated, declarer is sure to win ten tricks and fulfill his contract. He may now try for an extra trick by leading a Heart from dummy and playing low from his own hand. If it happens that the King of Hearts is in East's hand and will fall upon the next round, declarer will make five-odd, or one overtrick.

In this hand it will be seen that declarer should not draw trumps first. If he does he will not have sufficient trumps left in dummy to take care of his losing Diamonds.

The complete hand is:

NORTH

(Dummy)

♠ J 10 7 2

♡ Q 7 4

♢ 7

♣ A J 9 6 5

WEST

♠ K 4 3

♡ K 5 3

♢ K Q J 9 4

♣ 7 4

EAST

♠ Q 9 8 5

♡ 2

♢ 10 8 6 5

♣ K Q 10 8

SOUTH

(Declarer)

♠ A 6

♡ A J 10 9 8 6

♢ A 3 2

♣ 3 2

The next example is one in which declarer eliminates losers by discarding.

Dummy

♠ 8 6 4 3
♡ A Q J
◊ 6 5 2
♣ A 3 2

Declarer

♠ K Q J 10 9 5
♡ K
◊ A Q 4
♣ 9 6 4

The contract is 4 Spades. The opening lead by West is the Jack of Clubs. Declarer counts his losers as follows: in Spades, one; in Hearts, none; in Diamonds, two possible losers, for declarer may lose both the Queen and the four; in Clubs, two losers, for one of the Clubs is taken care of by dummy's Ace of Clubs. This is a total of five losers, so two of them must be eliminated.

Declarer wins the opening lead with the Ace of Clubs. And now, before drawing trumps, he must discard his losing Clubs. He therefore plays the Ace of Hearts, on which the King from his own hand falls. He then follows with the Queen of Hearts, discarding a small Club from his own hand; then the Jack of Hearts, discarding the remaining Club loser from his own hand. Declarer may then lead trumps, retaining the 5 of Spades in his own hand. When the Ace of Spades has been driven out, he will re-enter dummy by leading the 5 of Spades to the 8 in dummy, and will then lead a Diamond from dummy and finesse the Queen. When this finesse succeeds, he makes one overtrick.

The complete hand:

NORTH
(Dummy)
♠ 8 6 4 3
♡ A Q J
♢ 6 5 2
♣ A 3 2

WEST
♠ A
♡ 9 6 4 2
♢ 10 8 7 3
♣ J 10 8 7

EAST
♠ 7 2
♡ 10 8 7 5 3
♢ K J 9
♣ K Q 5

SOUTH
(Declarer)
♠ K Q J 10 9 5
♡ K
♢ A Q 4
♣ 9 6 4

The contract is 4 Spades on the following hand:

Dummy
♠ Q 10 9 3
♡ Q J 7 2
♢ 7 5
♣ A K 6

Declarer
♠ A K J 4
♡ K 5
♢ K 9 3 2
♣ 7 5 2

The opening lead is the Queen of Clubs, which is won in dummy with the King. Declarer now pauses to count his losers. In Spades, no losers; in Hearts, one loser—he must lose a trick to the Ace; in Diamonds, there is one certain loser to the Ace of Diamonds and one or two more possible losers in the small Diamonds; in Clubs, one loser. These must be reduced to three losers if South is to fulfill his contract.

In Hearts, if declarer's King is used to force out the Ace, the dummy will have two winners in the Queen and the Jack. On one of these South can discard the losing Club. Next comes the question whether trumps should be drawn. The answer is no, because South has Diamonds which he would like to trump in dummy with some of dummy's Spades. As for the Diamond suit, declarer should hope that East has the Ace, so that the King in his own hand can be established as a winner. Let us, therefore, begin with the actual play.

We have seen that South has just won the King of Clubs in dummy. His next play should be the Deuce of Hearts from dummy toward the King in the closed hand. Let us suppose that this holds the trick. A Heart should be returned immediately, and the Jack played from dummy. East wins with the Ace and returns a Club. West plays the 10, and South wins with the Ace in the dummy. The Queen of Hearts should now be played, and declarer discards his losing Club. Now it is time to work on the Diamond suit. Diamonds must be led from the dummy, else the opponents will surely win two Diamond tricks. The 7 of Diamonds is therefore played. East plays a small one, and South should go up with the King as his only chance to win a trick with that card. Fortunately, the King of Diamonds holds the trick, and a Diamond should be led back immediately so that the dummy will have no more of that suit. Now South will be in a position to trump two of his Diamonds in the dummy. He will lose, in all, only two tricks—the Ace of Diamonds and the Ace of Hearts—fulfilling his contract with an overtrick.

The complete hand is:

NORTH
(Dummy)
♠ Q 10 9 3
♡ Q J 7 2
◊ 7 5
♣ A K 6

WEST
♠ 7 5
♡ 9 8 6 3
◊ J 8 6
♣ Q J 10 4

EAST
♠ 8 6 2
♡ A 10 4
◊ A Q 10 4
♣ 9 8 3

SOUTH
(Declarer)
♠ A K J 4
♡ K 5
◊ K 9 3 2
♣ 7 5 2

Play at No Trump

Whereas in the play of a suit contract it is customary to count your losers at the start of play, it is better policy, when playing a No Trump contract, to count your winners. When you have bid 3 No Trump, you must try to win nine tricks.

Dummy	*Declarer*
♠ 7 5	♠ K J 6
♡ A J 4	♡ K Q
◇ A Q 8 3	◇ J 10 9 4
♣ J 10 9 5	♣ A Q 7 2

Declarer is playing a contract of 3 No Trump, and West leads the 4 of Spades. The 5 is played from dummy; East produces the Queen, which you, as South (declarer), win with the King.

You first count your immediate winners and find you have the one in Spades, which you have already taken; three in Hearts; the Ace of Diamonds; and the Ace of Clubs. These total six tricks. You must develop three more to fulfill your contract. You have the choice of developing these additional tricks in either Diamonds or Clubs by finessing against the King in both instances.

You must decide at this point which suit to work upon. Since you are in your own hand, it might seem convenient to lead the Jack of Diamonds in the hope that West has the King. In that ease you will win four Diamond tricks and be assured of your contract. However, if you try the Diamond finesse, and it loses to East, he will come through with a Spade. Your Jack will be captured, and West will run sufficient Spade tricks to defeat your contract. That is, East wins, let us say, with the King of Diamonds and leads back the 9 of Spades. What would you do? If you play the Jack, West will win with the Ace and his 10 of Spades will draw down your last Spade, the 6. If you play the 6, West will overtake with the 10 and your Jack will fall under the Ace. It is better, therefore, to try the Club finesse. If it should win, your troubles are over, for you will have nine tricks (one Spade, three Hearts, four Clubs, and the Ace of Diamonds). Even if the Club finesse should lose, you will not yet be down, because West will have the lead, and he will be unable to capture your Jack of Spades. For if West leads a Spade, you cannot be prevented from winning a trick with the Jack. He therefore must lead something else. This still gives you the opportunity to try the Diamond finesse; and this affords you two chances to win the hand.

The problem is, therefore, how to place the lead in the dummy in order to play the Jack of Clubs. The answer is that you lead the King or Queen of Hearts and overtake with the Ace in dummy. This is not wasting a trick, because you can win no more and no less than three tricks in Hearts, which you still retain. Upon overtaking the Heart in dummy, you then lead the Jack of Clubs.

The complete hand is as follows:

NORTH
(Dummy)
♠ 7 5
♡ A J 4
♢ A Q 8 3
♣ J 10 9 5

WEST
♠ A 10 8 4 2
♡ 9 6 5 3
♢ 6 2
♣ 8 4

EAST
♠ Q 9 3
♡ 10 8 7 2
♢ K 7 5
♣ K 6 3

SOUTH
(Declarer)
♠ K J 6
♡ K Q
♢ J 10 9 4
♣ A Q 7 2

As you will see, when the Club finesse wins, the nine tricks are assured.

Play by Defenders

If you have touching cards, when you are following suit, play the lower or lowest. But when you are leading, lead the higher or highest. (Exception: If the suit is headed by Ace-King, the King is played in either case.) For example:

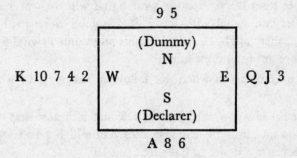

9 5

(Dummy)
N

K 10 7 4 2 W   E Q J 3

S
(Declarer)

A 8 6

Your partner, West, leads the 4 of Spades. You are East and should play the Jack, not the Queen. Don't act on the theory that "it makes no difference." It may not make any difference to you, but it will to partner. If you play the Jack and it forces South's Ace, West will know that you have the Queen. But if you play the Queen, and South wins with the Ace, your partner will not know the location of the Jack and may decline to lead the suit again, fearing that he might set up the Jack for South.

Bridge is a partnership game, and during the defense of a hand the partnership angle is extremely important. Sometimes, even with a completely useless hand, you may be of great assistance to your partner by giving him information he may need to conduct the defense. Messages can be conveyed to partner by means of the size of the card you play to various tricks. These are known as SIGNALS. The following examples will serve to illustrate the methods universally adopted for signaling:

The discard of an unnecessarily high card encourages partner to continue the suit led, and the discard of a low card discourages continuance of the suit. However, if you wish to encourage partner, you should signal with the highest card that you can afford.

If partner leads the Ace and you urgently desire the suit continued, assuming that you hold K-8-6-2, you should signal with the 8 rather than the 6, because your signal will then be more emphatic. If you signal with the 6, it might be understood by partner, but there might be a doubt in his mind. But a signal with the 8 is more apt to impress him.

Signals may be given when not following suit, that is, when discarding.

The discard of a low card from a side suit indicates that you do not wish that suit to be led. The discard of a high card from a side suit indicates a desire to have that suit led.

In discarding, when you play first a high card and then a low card, that amounts to a request for partner to lead that suit. To illustrate: If you discard first the 3 and then the 5, that indicates you have no desire to have that suit led; but if you discard first the 5 and then the 3, that would be known as a "come-on," asking partner to lead that suit.

Do not shift the lead from one suit to another unless you are sure that a change is indicated. In other words, normally we do not change horses in midstream. Unless you have good reason to the contrary, return your partner's suit.

Lead *through* strength. Lead *up to* weakness.

For example:

<pre>
                    ♠ J 10 8 4
                    ♡ A J 6 3
                    ◇ 6 5 3 2
                    ♣ 7

                    (Dummy)   ♠ 7 5 3
                       N   ♡ K Q 4
            W   E   ◇ 10 9 8
                       S   ♣ A 6 4 2
</pre>

Spades are trumps. You are East. Your partner, West, leads a Club which you win with the Ace. Let us assume that you wish to shift to a red suit (though perhaps a trump lead would be better). Note that the dummy has strength in Hearts and weakness in Diamonds. You should therefore lead "up to weakness," and choose the 10 of Diamonds. When your partner obtains the lead, it will be his turn to lead "through strength" (Hearts); and that will probably enable you to win two Heart tricks.

When declarer has trumps in both hands (his own and dummy's), do not lead a suit of which he is void in both hands, for that will permit him to trump in one hand, while on the same trick he discards a loser from the other hand.

Management of Hands on Defense

Let us examine the following illustrations to demonstrate the development of a hand both at suit play and at No Trump.

OBTAINING A RUFF

NORTH
(Dummy)
♠ A K Q
♡ J 10 9
◇ J 6 5 2
♣ 5 4 3

WEST
♠ 10 8 6
♡ 3 2
◇ 10 9 4 3
♣ K Q J 2

EAST
♠ 9 5 4 3 2
♡ 8 7 5
◇ A
♣ A 10 7 6

SOUTH
(Declarer)
♠ J 7
♡ A K Q 6 4
◇ K Q 8 7
♣ 9 8

South is declarer at a contract of 4 Hearts. West leads the King of Clubs, the top of his three-card sequence. The 3 is played from dummy. East, before playing to the first trick, plans the defense. In order to defeat the contract he and his partner must win four tricks. Partner's lead of the King announces possession of the Queen; so, if the defenders can cash the Ace, King, and Queen of Clubs, East's Ace of Diamonds will be the fourth, and setting, trick. However, it is more probable that after the Ace and King of Clubs are cashed, South, the declarer, will have no more Clubs, and will ruff. East therefore relies on winning only two tricks in Clubs. He can win the Ace of Diamonds, but that will total three tricks only—not enough to set the contract. However, if he can

arrange to get a ruff of a Diamond, the contract will be defeated.
If West is permitted to win the trick with the King of Clubs, he
will surely lead another Club. So East overtakes his partner's King
with his Ace, plays the Ace of Diamonds, and then leads back the
6 of Clubs. When West wins this trick with the Jack of Clubs, he
leads back a Diamond, and East ruffs for the fourth, and setting,
trick.

DUCKING TO MAINTAIN COMMUNICATION WITH PARTNER

NORTH
(Dummy)
♠ J 7 2
♡ 7 3
◇ A 10 6 4 3
♣ K J 4

WEST
♠ K 10 9 8 4
♡ J 6 4
◇ 8 7
♣ 10 9 7

EAST
♠ A 5 3
♡ K 10 9 5
◇ K 5 2
♣ 8 6 5

SOUTH
(Declarer)
♠ Q 6
♡ A Q 8 2
◇ Q J 9
♣ A Q 3 2

South is declarer at a contract of 3 No Trump. West leads the
10 of Spades. Resort to the opening-lead table will show this to

be the proper lead from this combination of cards. It is called the top of an inferior sequence. The Deuce is played from dummy. East wins with the Ace, and returns the 5 of Spades, the higher of his two remaining cards of that suit. The Queen is played by South. If West should take this trick, he would be in a position to drive out dummy's Jack of Spades and build up two good Spade tricks for himself. However, since he will never again be able to regain the lead, those two Spade tricks will be useless.

Since it is probable that East will obtain the lead again, it is wiser to permit East to retain a Spade, so that when East is again on lead, he can lead it. West accomplishes this by playing the 4 of Spades, permitting South to hold the second trick with the Queen.

Declarer cannot win nine tricks without taking at least two tricks in Diamonds. So he leads the Queen of Diamonds and lets it run. East wins with the King and returns a Spade, permitting West to take three more Spade tricks and thus defeat the contract.

GLOSSARY OF BRIDGE TERMS

Auction: The time when the bidding takes place.

Balanced Hand: A hand with 4-3-3-3, 4-4-3-2, or 5-3-3-2 distribution of the suits.

Bid: An offer to win a specified number of tricks. The bid may be made to win those tricks at No Trump, or the bid may be made as an offer to win a specified number of tricks with a suit as trumps.

Biddable Suit: A suit in order to be biddable must be at least four cards long and must be headed by at least 3 points—in other words, Q J x x or K x x x. Any five-card suit is biddable if it contains a face card.

Blackwood Convention: Under certain circumstances a bid of 4 No Trump requests partner to tell the number of Aces he has. This is used in connection with slam bidding.

Book: The first six tricks taken in by declarer. In other words, if the contract is to make 4 Spades, declarer must win ten tricks, since the first six tricks do not count toward the scoring. The term *book* is also used in connection with defenders. The defenders have taken their *book* when they have won all the tricks which the declarer can afford to lose and still fulfill his contract. For example, if the contract is 3 No Trump, the defenders' *book* is four tricks. As soon as they win another they have defeated the contract.

Buy the Contract: The highest bidder at the close of the auction is said to *buy the contract* for his side.

Call: A bid, double, redouble, or pass. In other words, any bid.

Cash: Taking a trick with a card.

Continue the Suit: This is an expression to describe the situation in which you have won a trick in a certain suit and return the same suit again.

Contractors: This is a term used to describe the players who made the final bid. The member of the contracting side who actually plays the hand is called *declarer* and his partner is the *dummy.*

Convention: This refers to a type of bid which by general agreement has a special, artificial meaning which might not seem natural on the surface.

Cover: To follow suit with a higher card.

Deal: To distribute the cards one at a time to the four players in rotation. The word *deal* is also used to describe the complete action on a hand, including the bidding and the play. For example, "We got a very good result on the last deal."

Dealer: The player whose turn it is to deal.

Deck (or Pack): The 52 Bridge cards.

Declarer: The member of the contracting side who actually plays his partner's cards (the dummy) as well as his own. The *declarer* is the member of the contracting side who first mentioned the suit which became the final trump; or, if it is a No Trump contract, he is the first member of the contracting side who bid No Trump.

Defeat the Contract: To prevent the declarer from winning the number of tricks bid for. Also: *"set the contract," "set the hand."*

Defenders: (1) During the bidding, the opponents of the opener. (2) During the play, the opponents of the declarer.

Defensive Bidding: Bidding by the opponents of the opening bidder.

Discard: A player *discards* when he is unable to follow suit and also when he fails to use a trump. The card which he plays is called a *discard.* Various words are employed which are synonymous with *discard.* Some of them are: *sluff, throw off.*

Double:

1. *Business Double:* A bid that indicates your belief that you can defeat your opponents.

2. *Take-out Double:* A bid which demands that your partner make a bid, if he has not already done so.

Double Raise: A raise from one to three or from two to four. In other words, raising one trick more than seems necessary. This is just as frequently referred to as a *jump raise.*

Doubleton: A holding of two cards of a suit.

Down: Failure to make contract. He is *down one* if he fails by one trick, *down two* if he fails by two tricks, etc.

Draw Trumps: To lead trumps until opponents have none left.

Duck: Playing a low card when you can, if you choose, play a higher one.

Entry, Re-entry: A trick-taking card that enables you to enter (or re-enter) the hand from which you wish to lead.

Finesse: An attempt to win a trick with a lower card when there is a higher one outstanding. For example, your dummy holds the Ace and Queen of a suit. The lead is in your own hand and you have two small cards. If you lead a small card to your dummy and play the Queen in the hope that it will win the trick, you are taking a *finesse.*

Forcing Bid: A bid demanding partner to keep the auction open. A bid may be forcing for one round, which means that partner must bid once more. And a bid may be forcing to game, which means that partner must keep bidding until a game contract is reached.

Free Bid: Any bid immediately after a bid by the right-hand opponent.

Fulfill the Contract: To win the number of tricks bid for. Synonyms: *make the contract; make the hand.*

Game: A score of 100 or more points below the line.

Grand Slam: The winning of all thirteen tricks.

Honor: An Ace, King, Queen, Jack, or 10.

Jump Bid: A bid higher than is needed to outbid the previous bid. For example, your partner bids 1 Heart and you respond 2 Spades. This is a *jump bid,* for you could have bid only 1 Spade had you chosen to.

Lead: (1) To play the first card of a trick. (2) The first card played to a trick.

Leader: The hand that plays the first card of any trick.

Little Slam: The winning of twelve tricks. Also called, Small Slam.

Loser: A card the opponents may win during the play.

Major Suit: Spades or Hearts.

Minor Suit: Diamonds or Clubs.

Opener: The player who makes the first bid. Also: *opening bidder, opening hand.*

Opening Bid: The first bid.

Opening the Bidding: To make the first bid.

Opening Lead: The lead to the first trick.

Overcall: A bid by an opponent of the opening bidder. For example, your right-hand opponent bids 1 Spade and you bid 2 Clubs. The 2-Club bid is an *overcall.*

Over-Ruff: To play a higher trump than one already played to the same trick.

Overtake: This refers to winning a trick your partner has already won. This you accomplish by playing a higher card than he has played.

Overtrick: Each trick won in excess of those contracted for.

Part Score: A score of less than 100 points below the line. (A bid of 3 Spades or 4 Clubs will not produce a game regardless of how many tricks declarer wins.)

Pass: A bid indicating that player does not wish to enter the auction at this point.

Penalties: Points scored above the line as a result of defeating a contract.

Penalty Double: (see: *Double*) A double made for the purpose of scoring the high penalties awarded to defenders for defeating a doubled contract. Synonym: *business double.*

Picture Cards: Aces, Kings, Queens and Jacks. These are also referred to as *face cards.* While the 10 is an honor card, nevertheless it is not referred to as a *face card.*

Pre-emptive Bid: An unnecessarily high bid (3, 4, or 5) intended to make it difficult for opponents to enter the bidding. Also called a *shut-out bid.*

Raise: You *raise* your partner's bid by making a higher bid in the same suit. For example, your partner bids 1 Spade and you bid 2 Spades. That is a *raise.* But if you bid 2 Hearts, that would not be a *raise,* but a take-out. Synonymous with the term *raise* are *assist* and *support.*

Rebid: A player's second or subsequent bid.

Rebiddable Suit: A five-card suit headed by at least two high honors. This means that it may, if necessary, be bid a second time without support from partner. Any six-card suit, or longer, is rebiddable.

Redouble: A bid indicating player's belief that his side *can* make the bid just doubled by opponents.

Responder: The partner of the opening bidder.

Response: The first bid by the opener's partner.

Rubber: When a side has won two games.

Ruff: To play a trump when another suit is led. This can be done only when ruffer is unable to follow suit.

Sequence: Two or more cards held in one hand ranking next to each other.

Set: To defeat. This is synonymous with *defeat* or *put down.*

Show out: Fail to follow suit.

Side Suit: A suit of at least 4 cards, other than the trump suit, in the declarer's hand or in the dummy.

Singleton: An original holding of one card of a suit.

Underbid: A bid which does not reveal the full strength of a hand.

Void: No cards of a suit. Synonym: *blank suit.*

Vulnerable: A side is *vulnerable* after winning its first game of a rubber.

A Note about the Author

CHARLES H. GOREN is the Number One ranking player of the United States in the official ratings of the American Contract Bridge League. He holds virtually every record of note on the books of tournament play. He has won more National Championships than anyone in history and holds the record for the most number of National Championships won in a single year (five). Incidentally, he is the only player in the history of Bridge who has ever won every major championship in the United States.

Mr. Goren's daily column is syndicated in 150 newspapers which have a combined circulation of over twenty-five million. This makes it, of course, the most widely distributed Bridge column in the history of the game.

His books have been translated into French, Spanish, Swedish, and enjoy wide publication throughout the British Empire. His recent book, *Point Count Bidding,* published by Simon and Schuster, is the most successful Bridge book in the last fifteen years and has changed the bidding habits of millions of players throughout the United States and Europe.

The point count method introduced by Mr. Goren several years ago has now been adopted by all recognized authorities of the game.